Wink at
SUCCESS
Flirt With
SERENITY

An Affirmative Guide
to Personal Peace

by Dennis Alcorn

Blue Canoe Publishing

Dallas, Texas

Published by:
Blue Canoe Publishing
5823 Boca Raton
Dallas, TX 75230

Library of Congress Cataloging-in-Publication Data

Alcorn, Dennis R.
Wink at Success, Flirt with Serenity
1. Success 2. Self-Improvement 3. Recovery

LC No. 92-73377

ISBN 0-9633857-0-4

Grateful acknowledgement is made to Linda Carrara for permission to reprint "The Wind", written on the banks of Round Pond.

Expressed appreciation to the following for their editorial assistance: Linda Carrara, Phil Eagleton, Pat Fluekiger and Debby Wilberger

Cover Design and Layout by Michael Morris Design, Inc.
Calligraphy by Susie-Melissa Cherry

Copies of calligraphic quotes may be ordered from:
Blue Canoe Publishing

Acknowledgements

A few years ago, life presented me with changes, and I began a new journey. These and others have made an unforgettable contribution to my healing, growth and joy, resulting in the writing of this book. For this, I am eternally grateful.

To my Mother and Father for the gifts of their heritage; my brother, David, for being so incredibly cool; and my sister, Fawn, for helping me make it through the rain.

To Robin G. for knowing when to show me a new path; Marilyn P. for showing me how to talk with my Creator; P.J. for being there; Aunt Marlynn for simply knowing, and letting me grieve.

To S.II Group for inspiration, healing and love; Dick M. for genuine male friendship and understanding; Joanie P. for demonstrating dependable long distance friendship; Paul Bowles and Sylvia Peterson for gentle support, guidance and discovery; Susie Q. for teaching me about storms; Brandie for saying hello again.

To Lady Linda C., my best friend during this writing, for wanting to give me the love I want; and always, to my Higher Power for letting me know.

To all those seeking the lost joy in themselves,
and

To Little Den.

Table of Contents

Forward

Absolutely thrilled! That was the feeling I experienced after reading Dennis Alcorn's book. Let me explain why.

Most people seek therapy because they think they are in some way a failure and they feel powerless. They believe that success is the key to feeling powerful and the answer to happiness. And they're right; success is the answer to happiness - but only when the sense of power arising from success is a feeling of personal potency arising from within one's self.

The myth of success is the idea that material possessions, status, strength and control of people and situations brings certainty to life. Success might be labeled "addiction to social conformity." If you believe this myth - and most people in our culture do - then you are bestowing on things and people other than yourself the ability - the power - to give or take away your own personal potency: your SELF.

Competition for this projected image of success is often fierce, and the results can be tragic. Most tragic of all is the fact that you are fighting a losing battle, because you can't have enough material possessions, status, strength and control of people and situations to generate that inner sense of personal potency - which is the only source of real serenity, peace and happiness. Toxic shame is the end result because toxic shame is the result of a social crime, the disobeying of a social law.

Dennis Alcorn precipitates us into a new interface: the relationship between success and serenity. He teaches us in a progression of steps how to "wink at success and flirt with serenity." He clearly defines how there are no mistakes or failures in life - only lessons to be learned. I can't think of anything more important to our peace and happiness than learning how serenity breeds success.

We need this book and we need it badly because people in our culture feel a deep need for society's measure of success. All who read this book have one fundamental thing in common: All are human and the one essential ingredient for success is to feel and "BE" human. Thanks, Dennis, for showing us how.

Sylvia Ogden Peterson
author of
From Love That Hurts To Love That's Real

Preface

Since the beginning, we have all wanted to be successful. And we want success on our own terms. Many times we achieve the success we've defined for ourselves only to find that we don't FEEL successful. We're not content, we have no peace of mind or serenity.

Success is difficult to define. It's like trying to define Love or God or a Miracle. But each of us is entitled to define success as we understand it. The purpose of this book is to provide an easy, gentle guide to defining success for yourself, starting on the road to that success, and maintaining some sensibility, some peace while on that road.

Most of the guidance available on achieving success suggests that we follow certain steps that will take us to our dreams. Though some have merit, the difficulty with many of these strategies is that they create a one dimensional path ... one that can create obsessive behaviors. Recent discovery tells us that despite all the guidance and motivation available at bookstores and seminars, there are roadblocks caused by childhood wounds, emotional trauma and compulsive or obsessive behaviors that prevent us from getting what we want out of life.

This book was written so that those confused or frustrated by the traditional "personal power" or "success formula" publications and the more recent discoveries about healing obsessive behaviors and finding spirituality, can find along with me a way to establish a peaceful harmony between the two concepts ... a balance.

Together we can learn how to have personal success and feel the joy and rapture that is rightfully ours. Through the gentle exploration of our awareness and beliefs, universal concepts of Nature, choices and Calculated Life Management, we can learn how to be in that state of living that satisfies our ambition and ego while comforting our consciousness and connecting us to all things peaceful.

My personal life experiences, including many successes and failures in all areas, led me to believe that there is a way to have success without an "all or nothing" attitude, without having to set inflexible goals that cause anxiety, and despite learned behaviors and emotional myths. Prior to "awakening", my concept of success was blurred by the notions that I should just push, push, push, control everything, never acknowledge my feelings and never give myself a break. Peace of mind was a completely foreign concept that frankly, didn't fit in with my kind of "ambition". And, while I experienced success, I felt disconnected and separate from the rest of the world. Regardless of my success, I really didn't feel like I belonged and my "failures" were particularly difficult to accept.

What I really want is success AND serenity. As I come to have the success I desire, I want also to remain connected to my inner self and to other people important to me. I want that lifespark that connects us all to burn brightly and consistently.

1

The Inevitable Journey

Success is personal and it is a choice.

Most of the popular literature on success addresses several "keys" to success or "habits" that must be developed in order to achieve success. They often subscribe to very specific attitudes or formulas that can result in a somewhat contrived "burning desire". Most often, the goal is to create a drive within you that can best be described as an obsession.

This book is not about creating obsession. Obsession is unhealthy and certainly would stand in the way of any flirtation with serenity.

Traditional definitions of success often refer to the accumulation of materialistic wealth. Other descriptions reference the more cerebral sense of success. One image promises you can languish on your large estate, collecting exotic and expensive cars; investments earning high returns and your company shooting onto the Fortune 500. The second image has you sitting on a mountaintop in a yoga-like position unconcerned about money because you are at one with the universe.

I contend that there is a middle ground and these definitions do not have to be mine or yours. Success should be defined for yourself by you and only you. Most of us want to create our own lifestyle and our own peace without dropping out. We still want to participate in the real world.

That's the subject of this book. It's about the process of living successfully in spite of our past and despite our circumstances. We can recover from learned myths and live peacefully within the real parameters of everyday life. During the process, we discover what we want out of life and how to get it without giving up our 'self' along the way. We examine the process of putting ourselves in a place of serenity while moving towards a level of achievement that has been defined by each of us. A place that we design, not a place we find through someone else's formula or by accident because we're acting out our predetermined destiny. There may be a master plan beyond our control, but we can choose to captain our own ship. Today, we can choose not to be a result of our past and to consciously explore the choices for our future.

The concepts in the following pages provide ways to view life, to view ourselves, to view others, to synthesize information already available to us, to recognize destructive behavior and to establish healthy behavior. We learn to choose balance, to evaluate alternate futures and to establish spiritual relationships with our God, ourselves and our universe. If this sounds idealistic, grandiose or pretentious, don't be concerned. We will explore "real stuff" — not stuff that is necessarily subjective or esoteric. To wink at success and flirt with serenity is a viewpoint that recognizes the realities and practicalities of life with a knowing smirk. We acquire knowledge and acceptance of ourselves that can be realized by following a particular, yet flexible path. This rather adventurous exploration allows us to discover our own beliefs, establish new behaviors and apply them to a future we choose. Most importantly, we give ourselves permission to succeed and have fun along the way.

The Circumstances of Life

We begin with understanding the circumstances of life. In his widely read book, *The Road Less Traveled*, Scott Peck begins by saying that "Life is difficult". I'm more comfortable acknowledging that the CIRCUMSTANCES of life are difficult. It is my perception of these circumstances that can make my life difficult. Life just is.

To complicate matters, the circumstances of life always change. There are inevitable twists and turns, ups and downs, rights and lefts, joys and sorrows. And it's going on right now. We have to be in it. This may not be the final performance, but neither is it a dress rehearsal. As John Lennon once said, "Life is what happens to you while you are busy making other plans". So it is more a matter of how we choose to deal with these ever changing circumstances that determines our success in life.

The only thing preventing each of us from being a success as we understand it is our perception of self and our perception of the journey of life. It's not the circumstances. We're not victims of our circumstances, our circumstances are a victim of our perception. In other words, it is not our circumstances that cause us pain or pleasure, it is our chosen response to our circumstances that causes us pain or pleasure. This explains why certain people seem to "rise above" an experience or circumstance. They do not perceive themselves as victims. Rather, they perceive the circumstance as an opportunity or, at least, as a situation that does not limit the enjoyment of the rest of their life. Their "problems" are ultimately perceived as "teachers". Our perception of self is dependent on our willingness to gently remove the mental and emotional roadblocks that are in the way of our natural path to success.

Accepting Change

Many of us find it difficult to accept the dynamics of life. We are resistent to everything going on around us. Yet, everything around us is changing - people, circumstances, the environment. Often, what is true today can be false tomorrow. Why do we remain so rigid? Why do we look for black and white? Why can't we move with the winds of change? Perhaps because we're taught that there is right and wrong, left and right, north and south, up and down, supply and demand. While that applies to technology and some rudimentary principles in the world, it doesn't necessarily apply to the process of life. Anything living changes or grows, and is subject to the changing dynamics around it. Change requires an awareness and acceptance of the forces in all that matters. To remain rigid and not change is a direct affront to Nature and all that is known.

Nature is a supreme model for all of us. Nature tells us that life is a series of planting and harvesting, high tides and low tides, sunrises and sunsets, holding on and letting go, births, deaths and fortunately, rebirths. Nature tells us that there will be unplanned happenings. To flirt with serenity, we can observe Nature. Change is natural. It is resistance to change that's traumatic.

Students of success and serenity find it inherently necessary to accept that change will be in their lives. Now this doesn't mean we just blindly accept with resignation that life is a pain. Accepting circumstances does not mean we have a negative or "expect the worse" attitude toward life. To the contrary, it simply means we accept that the winds of change are always blowing and that their whole purpose is to urge us to accommodate the inevitable dance of life. Then, we get to choose the music.

Haven't we all heard someone say, "I knew it was coming", or "I had a feeling", or "At some level, I really knew what was going to happen." I've often said to myself, "All the signs were there". We seem to have the innate knowledge that circumstances will change and may not always be pleasant.

We can accept that the circumstances of life are difficult and change is inevitable. The recognition and acceptance that there will be problems is to flirt with serenity. A very good friend used this imagery to explain it:

You hear it coming before it ever
    reaches you.
You can see the far off tree tops
    quiver in the fading sun.
Suddenly you feel, smell, and hear
    it—

        —The Wind—

The roar then fades off in the
    distance
       as it continues its journey.
A journey whose sole purpose is
    to make leaves
       dance.

State of Flow

You may be saying to yourself that you know there will problems. But what's really needed is an ACCEPTANCE that there will be problems. Knowledge and acceptance are different. We may acknowledge that there will be problems in life, but accepting means giving up the fantasy that serious problems only happen to others, or that we'll never "go through that again". While applying our efforts towards achieving success, we must accept the twists and turns with grace. I call it being in a State of Flow.

Many of us tend to focus on events, achievements and what's next. Being in a State of Flow is a state of mind that focuses on the journey, the moving picture, the whole ball field, and taking it as it comes. Flowing through life does not mean being lackadaisical, or limiting our participation or ambition. Rather, because we are in a state of flow, we can actually participate more willingly and move through the twists and turns without serious injury.

What we resist, persists.
When we flow, it will go.

Choosing a State of Flow is not always easy. It requires real awareness to observe not only what goes on "around" me, but what goes on "with" me. Real awareness is "thinking about what I'm thinking about". That is, I must have a detached thought process of observing my own actions and reactions to what is going on around me — and, consciously and deliberately, make a personal choice to flow.

So, if we recognize that the circumstances of life are constantly changing and that we can accommodate those changes by being in a State of Flow, we can begin to recognize that success is really a process, specifically, a natural process. And, that process includes those events that are traditionally referred to as failures or mistakes.

Reframing Success and Failure

Serenity cannot be realized without the acceptance of mistakes and outcomes that are unpleasant. In this context, acceptance does not mean that we have to like what happened, nor do we deny our feelings about the outcome. But, we need not obsess about the outcome, rather view it is as part of the bigger, moving picture ... life. It is not our whole life and it need not affect our tomorrow. For it is from those mistakes and negative happenings that we are able to build as we strive for success. Throughout history, it seems that pain and "failure" almost always precede greatness.

For the purposes of this book, I have reframed the traditional views of success and failure. Success and failure are merely labels given to an outcome. In both cases, the outcomes are a result of some vision I developed and action I have taken. Every action has a consequence. Sometimes, those consequences are in harmony with my expectations, sometimes they are not. Success and failure as a concept, relate more to my individual perception than to any specific rule or definition. The outcome of my vision is determined by my specific objectives and the way I approach them, rather than some dogmatic standards established by other people.

Success is merely the perception of a favorable outcome. Failure is something we perceive as an unfavorable outcome, something we wish had turned out better, a learning experience. To "deal with" or "process" an unfavorable outcome, we start by noticing our feelings, becoming aware of how we are handling the situation, our actions and, most important, reactions. We grieve the outcome. It's okay to feel bad or sad about it. That's how we get in touch with ourselves and flirt with serenity. We accept that the outcome IS and there is nothing left but the learning. We plan how to handle similar experiences in the future. Finally, we return to a State of Flow, no longer dwelling on what has gone or what will be, but returning to the present.

When asked about a "failure", a good response is "Well, that didn't turn out like I had hoped, but I learned from it and the experience is contributing to my success today." By accepting this definition, I never really "fail". I reflect that it had an outcome less favorable than what I had hoped for, but I learned from it. And, there is recognition that the learning from that outcome was necessary for me to grow toward my understanding of success. Knowing that these learning experiences are a part of success, I can wink at success quite often.

There is great wisdom in learning not to suffer from failure. When asked about her success, Barbra

Streisand stated that what makes her different is that she is willing to experience failure. Thomas Edison winked at success ten thousand times on his way to inventing a light bulb that worked. Babe Ruth set a record for the most strikeouts on the way to his home run record. On our way to each incredible success, most of us will set records for learning experiences.

Failure Provides Opportunity

We can benefit by keeping in mind that every "failure" or learning experience is a prelude to an opportunity. Something good will come of it. Everything has a consequence. There are offsetting positives and negatives. Admittedly, the offsetting consequence is sometimes subtle and may not appear immediately. But it will come. It's a natural law.

Mistakes are not setbacks, but rather a necessary step forward. It's okay to make mistakes. You can reframe your view of a mistake. Making a mistake doesn't mean you are a mistake. You're still you. Mistakes are like the rough edges of a diamond. Each time we "polish" an edge, the closer we are to the finished diamond. We can't have a beautiful diamond without polishing the rough edges, and enjoying the polishing process helps create serenity.

Success and failure are part of the same process, not exclusive happenings. Failure is part of the process of success. In fact, it's not likely we will ever achieve success without failure. Many people achieve their greatest success after what is known as "hitting bottom" or what they see as their greatest failure.

That is when their life reaches a place where they find the personal and spiritual strength to begin to make choices that result in positive outcomes.

Everyone has their own "bottom". There are many stories of how people have achieved great success after a crippling injury. One inspiring example among many is the story of Terry Fox, author of *The Other Side of the Mountain*. Others may hit bottom after losing an important job or relationship. But, even those that hit bottom continue to experience life's ups and downs. It's just that their bottoming out experience often teaches them acceptance. We will not have favorable outcomes without unfavorable ones - learning experiences. It is that way.

The Ultimate Success, A Definition

I define the Ultimate Success in life as progressive growth and acceptance of natural outcomes, both favorable and unfavorable, resulting in feelings of self-approval, oneness and peace of mind. Success is not represented by a place or reward or result or destination. It's an experience, a viewpoint, a state of mind. The acceptance of outcomes and the state of flowing through them sets up a flirtation with serenity. This definition implies an ongoing "journey" and an ongoing "effort", and "allows" me to calmly deal with the circumstances that come my way. If I can claim self-approval, be connected to others, and have peace of mind, I can sustain a mental, emotional and spiritual fitness that encompasses all areas of my life including family, friends, business and finances.

How do we get into a State of Flow? How do we begin this "new" and "natural" journey towards success and serenity? We may have discovered several obstacles or "roadblocks" that are preventing us from gaining that viewpoint. We may have certain behaviors or compulsions that keep us from flirting with serenity. In the following chapters, we will discuss ways we can overcome those roadblocks, and wink and flirt and wink and flirt...

Most of the roadblocks have to do with fear. And fear is difficult to manage without a belief system.

2
Believe In Yourself,
and Soon
The World Will Follow

Those may be the most important words in this book.

Many of us have been exposed to the philosophies of great motivators about the merits of a positive mental attitude. And, beyond any doubt, what we choose to think or believe is the single most determining factor in our success.

However, my concern is that the words "positive mental attitude" have become so overused that they have lost true meaning. Some would have us believe that if we simply say we have a positive attitude then we will. If we get up in the morning, look in the mirror and tell ourselves it's a great day, everything will work out well. That may be over-simplified, but you're familiar with the concept.

Belief, the Foundation

I suggest that the real foundation of attitude is belief. Belief is the internalization of an attitude. Internalization means it becomes a part of you. Attitude seems to be centered on intellectual or conscious thought. Unfortunately, many of the messages we have received that have caused pain or discomfort in our lives have been internalized. That is, we think "on automatic" or worse, we don't even think. We are not consciously aware of our thoughts. Therefore, we just react. Our behavior has been programmed...by others as well as ourselves. For example, as a child, Janet, a computer whiz, received covert messages from her father that she wasn't capable of any real intellectual accomplishment, and she had better take advantage of her good looks. Now, each time her boss expresses his appreciation for a job well done, she automatically "discounts" her accomplishment as "no big deal", minimizing her special ability to assimilate numerical information. Instead, she quickly straightens her blouse and brushes back her hair, unconsciously hoping to receive his approval for her physical "presentation".

So, how does one become a believer? How do we examine and change some of our old beliefs? Frankly, it's not easy. If it were, you wouldn't see this or any other self-help book on the shelves at your local bookstore. Actually, we find it difficult to believe that good things can happen. We automatically believe that bad will occur, or that we are not worthy of good things.

Old Messages, Old Beliefs

The reason we unconsciously think negatively is that we have received so many messages suggesting that we "can't, won't, didn't, weren't, aren't and haven't", that we believe it. Or, these often subtle messages tell us we are "okay, only if...". The little child that lives within each of us "holds on" to these messages forever. These often subtle messages are "transmitted" to us and forever stored in our computer-like brains by the time we are six or seven years old. We have internalized these messages. Despite our well-intended parents, relatives, siblings and friends, these messages are often a compilation of their own spiritual and emotional wounds from past generations. In Janet's situation, most likely her father got the message from his primary caretakers that "the way you look" is more important than "the way you are".

It's extremely important to remember that many of these behavioral messages started generations ago and were passed on unconsciously and unceremoniously. It is not beneficial to blame anyone in particular, but rather, simply acknowledge that the "scripts" are there. And in addition to the self-destructive behaviors, we can acknowledge that many of these "inherited" behaviors are very positive ... gifts from our heritage.

The passing on of these behavioral wounds results in the creation of our own fears and behavioral triggers. Unless we make an excruciating and calculated choice not to believe or respond to the old "programming", these "built in" responses will remain in our subconscious and we will have to deal with them for the rest of our lives. You see, we will have beliefs. They will be ours, or those of someone else.

The messages or "scripts" we have heard over and over in our lifetimes are like old 78 rpm records stored forever in the recesses of our minds. Even as we go through adult life, many of them are played repeatedly so we hear the message over and over and over.

27

Eventually that message is internalized and we act on it from an unconscious level, even though sometimes our gut or instinct says differently. Unless we are extremely aware of the signals, we don't even know when something we are doing goes against our instinct. We just feel "funny" and then go ahead without further reflection. To put it a different way, whatever we learned to do, or be, when we were growing up will continue to influence our behaviors as adults until we can identify the old messages, have feelings about them, recognize their effect and make conscious decisions to change.

For example, as I grew up I developed a belief that it mattered more what other people thought than what I thought. Almost everything I did was an effort to be acknowledged by others. My identity came from the outside in. My self-esteem came from a dependency on others for approval. I was a "performer". I did not know what my own feelings were, only what I thought I "should" do to get the approval of others. I used to "should" on myself a lot.

Eventually, I needed to feel like I was in control of "everything" so that "everything" would look good so that "everybody" would like me. Truly, I became dependent on and addicted to other people. This led to efforts to control the people and events around me so that nothing would go "wrong" and I would never be perceived as anything less than special. I "believed" that it was my responsibility to make sure everything was okay, to fix everything. I became centered on everyone elses feelings and outcomes. This led to some "caretaking" and "people pleasing" behaviors that shut down my ability to experience my own feelings. I "medicated" my feelings by becoming an acquisition and achievement addict...all in an effort to get the approval of others.

During those times, my achievement addiction led to some great "success". Yet, I was emotionally and spiritually unsettled and didn't know why. I had not yet learned how to wink at success or flirt with serenity. This continuous effort to control and "perform as a god" led to still more rigid behavior, perfectionism and high anxiety.

These behaviors alienated people I cared about, because in an effort to control, I was covertly trying to sabotage their identity. The result was that I contributed to the destruction of relationships I cherished. Ultimately, I lost my self. I had no identity of my own and experienced a lot of emotional pain until I was able to identify how I got those "control everything" messages, until I was able to have feelings of anger and sadness about the losses I suffered while acting out those behaviors, and until I was able to begin letting go of the old scripts and gently begin to discover the real me. Only then could I experience the freedom of having my own feelings, my own identity and my own belief system. Only then was I able to develop supportive, nurturing relationships that allowed "everyone" to succeed or fail on their own. As a postscript, I am now experiencing my greatest success - in every part of my life.

I believe the instinct that helps us rid ourselves of harmful learned behaviors is one that is spiritual. It's that universal belief seed planted in each of us that gives us the capability of knowing what is best for ourselves. The key is to listen. Not listening to ourselves and telling ourselves we don't deserve what we want and need keeps us from getting the information necessary to make good choices.

To overcome that old programming is an awesome task, because by the time we are adults, we act out these old "built in" scripts automatically. To change these scripts takes an awareness that things aren't working the way we want them to, or that we don't like the results we keep getting each time we behave a certain way. Not an easy task, because many of us believe that we can't manage these old scripts. The truth is that our beliefs are the only thing we can manage. We are powerless over all other people, places and things. But, our Creator did give us the ability to question, reflect, review, ponder, contemplate, challenge and choose the way we believe. What a gift! It's called free will.

A quick wink at success means we ask ourselves, where did I get that belief? Is it really what I believe, or am I acting or reacting out of someone else's programming?

We can create new messages. It's like recording new Compact Discs with "new and improved" messages. Messages that can be played today, not old 78's from yesterday. If we choose, we can even record some of the old messages on the new CD, if we honestly feel those beliefs are empowering in our life today.

Having used this analogy, I don't mean to imply that with a snap of our fingers we can change a belief. For now, we can just be aware that we have the choice.

If nothing changes, nothing changes.
If anything changes, everything changes.
If I won't change, I don't change.
I changed and my life changed.

The incredible thing about changing beliefs is that, despite all the help, guidance, rules and reasons to adopt a positive belief system, it's still personal. I am the only one that can do it for me. That is why most people that are able to change or "turn their lives around" do so when they hit bottom ... when they come to believe they have no choice but to experience a catharsis of their old beliefs.

But, it doesn't always have to be that way. We can each choose at any time to see the positive, to see the possibilities and to believe that we can accomplish anything we desire. However, we must accept that we are the ones responsible. No one else can be responsible for our beliefs or attitudes. And, we are the only ones who can choose to see the other side, to wink at success.

We can't expect anyone else to cause us to succeed. We can stand right next to the most positive, successful person in the world and it will not magically rub off on us.

That's not to say we can't learn from the success of others. It's highly desirable and well documented that we can model both success and failure. We can copy the habits of others, act out those behaviors and achieve our goals. But recognize that it is still up to us to choose to believe that we can copy success.

Imagination, the Parent of Belief

A new belief is born of imagination. We first imagine what we can be, or accomplish, or have, before we can believe. It becomes clear that if we can't picture these things, we won't be able to develop a viewpoint, create an attitude and internalize a belief. So we start by imagining. In this case, imagining does not mean projecting or living in the future. We're talking about imagining a state of mind. Imagining that we can have the feeling, be the person, do the task. Richard Bach states in his book, *One,* that "No matter how qualified or deserving we are, we will never reach a better life until we can imagine it for ourselves and allow ourselves to have it."

Once you can imagine a certain state of being, you can begin to develop an attitude from an intellectual standpoint that it is possible. Your "new" brain can rationalize that it could be...that it might happen...that you possibly can. This is a very conscious effort requiring a genuine desire on your part to have things in your life be different. Sometimes this only happens when you BELIEVE you have no choice. But, you always do. This time, you think "What have I got to lose?" Or perhaps someone said something that encouraged you and planted a small seed of possibility in the garden of your imagination.

*The first step to having all you want
is to imagine
having all you want.*

Changing Belief Patterns

The next step in developing a belief system is to take a small action towards the new belief. Rather than waiting until you feel you can make a dramatic and complete change in your beliefs, just do something small in the right direction. It doesn't require all the courage in the world. Just a little; the courage of a small child. It may sound trite, but try a little "baby step". As a fortune cookie I once read said, "He who waits to do a great deal of good at once will never do anything". For example, I've discovered you don't just "write a book", you start with a sentence.

Robert, a middle management executive, had trouble confronting or even talking to his boss. To begin to change his beliefs about talking with superiors, he first imagined a comfortable, intellectually stimulating and mutually beneficial meeting to discuss project management with his boss. He then developed a strategy that started with just greeting the boss in the morning with a handshake, a smile, a look in the eye and a "good morning". Though that may seem rather simplistic, it's the way to begin to change a belief system because now Robert's brain and the little child within him has new evidence, an affirming result, that he CAN talk to the boss. And, he can now begin to internalize that belief, although on a very low level.

Now Robert could take a second action based on his imagined situation and his intellectual attitude. The second action will be affirming as well and again sends new messages to his brain. He can start up a casual conversation with his boss regarding a current project. Initially, he determined it should be a conversation that does not require any decision making, one that is non-threatening. A conversation regarding the current status of a project already under way and one in which Robert was not critically involved seemed to work well. With this pattern repeated over and over in a progressive manner, Robert's imagination, intellect, actions and affirming result, installed in his subconscious a new internalized belief that talking to his boss was possible.

It takes at least three to five actions to BEGIN the internalization process. If you find that on occasion, you don't quite get the results you hoped for, flow through that event (flirt with serenity), and start again with imagination, intellectual attitude, small non-threatening steps, new affirming result and new belief. Many experts suggest that it takes at least twenty-one days to develop a new habit or belief. To wink at success, we accept that even new beliefs will need repeated application over time or they will go away. The old messages nudge their way back in, or we are once again exposed to old messages. Even though we live in a state of flow, we do not lose consciousness, but remain consciously aware that our chosen beliefs need reinforcement.

Remember that your imagination must always be the parent of each effort to change or establish a belief. None of the world's great accomplishments would have come about without someone first imagining that it could be. The pattern will look something like this:

Imagine

Intellectual Attitude (Conscious)

1st Action

Affirming Result

Belief (Level 1, Unconscious Doubt)

2nd Action

Affirming Result

Belief (Level 2, Conscious Internalization)

More Action

Affirming Result

Belief (Level 3, Unconscious Internalization)

Three Necessary Beliefs

There are three fundamental beliefs that form a solid foundation for all others. The first is belief in your Supreme Creator. With that belief, you can know that you don't have to do it alone. It feels good to know that a godly strength is available to you. Flirting with serenity is simply not possible without a spiritual relationship with your God. This does not necessarily call for a specific religion, institution or dogma. Rather, your spirituality can be personal. Again, believe in YOUR Supreme Creator.

We each have the right to develop our own sense of God, as we understand Him. We can call Him a Higher Power, God, our Creator, Lord, Jesus, Buddha, the Master Planner, the Force or whatever. But it is important to have a comfortable and personal spirituality. I found it helpful to free myself from any forced or judgmental doctrine and imagine a gentle God with whom I would be comfortable. This concept is not meant to be irreverent, sacrilegious or disrespectful. Instead, it is freeing and spiritual, and can harmonize with any religion. If you are comfortable with your current beliefs, and they are really yours, then that's great. I started with a belief that my Spiritual Guide is a gentle energy flowing through all things, willing and available to comfort me, guide me and love me unconditionally. From there, my belief has grown to accept that my Higher Power is a friendly guide that can heal me, protect me, remind me, show me the way, keep me grounded and balanced, and grant me gifts when I least expect it.

Though it may be difficult at first, I invite you to discover your own spiritual guide. One that you can look to without fear of judgement and without fear of consequences. You can develop that spirituality that you can call on for strength at any time knowing that you are ultimately safe. You can trust that your Higher Power has a plan and only asks that you do the footwork, that you participate in the process. Then, your spirituality can be made a part of you. And, don't forget that you can change your belief. Your beliefs can change, grow and be flexible. After all, it is YOUR belief.

If you have difficulty getting started on the journey of discovering your spirituality, there is help. When someone is spiritually bankrupt, I strongly recommend one of the most effective ways to begin the search is in a healthy 12-step program. Based on the principles founded in Alcoholics Anonymous, these programs now address other compulsive or addictive behaviors such as co-dependency, over-eating, spending, work, love and sex. The environment is anonymous, safe, free, non-denominational and allows you to develop your own understanding of God. These programs have a proven system for the discovery and recovery of your principles, your identity and your place in the universe. Simply, these programs are unique. Though there is a kind and gentle path of guidance, the program offers the ultimate choice for your own personal needs and growth. They can supplement your existing religious or spiritual beliefs and offer one of the safest places known to make discoveries related to spirituality.

Once you have established some spirituality, you can now begin to approach the belief that will carry you towards success: belief in yourself.

Believe in yourself, and soon the world will follow. We can choose to believe in ourselves in THIS moment, THIS time. It doesn't matter what we believed in the past, or what we felt about ourselves in the past. This is today. This is the only moment that matters.

On Being Worthy

As we learn to examine our behaviors, we discover that many of us got old messages, many of them covert, that stated we were worthy *only if...* or, we were not worthy *unless...* . These messages were actually telling us that we could only feel good about ourselves under certain conditions. Conditions that were usually dictated by someone else's beliefs. These beliefs did not give us the freedom to like or respect ourselves. So, we spend the rest of our lives trying to "erase" the *only if*. We go to extraordinary measures to get that ultimate, unconditional approval, which can really only come from within.

Despite all the conditional messages that many of us grew up with and continue to receive on a regular basis, each of us is a worthy person. We are worthy of success and serenity. We are worthy of being in this world and having the life we want. Unfortunately, it is incredible how few of us are able to generate a gut level, or instinctual, belief in ourselves. We search for our worth everywhere but within ourselves - from our mates, our children, our grades in school, our boss, how much money we make, the car we drive, the clothes we wear and on and on. Though having the respect of others and a feeling of accomplishment is desirable, it's not what makes us worthy.

Belief that those external forces create our worth is what makes it difficult to flow through life with serenity. We cannot always control external forces. If belief in yourself is dependent on things outside yourself, you will spend most of your time disappointed and feeling unworthy of success. Believe in yourself, and soon the world will follow. You choose your life. Start with a conscious belief that you can succeed, that you are worthy and that you belong.

A good way to develop a belief system in yourself is to create a "sales presentation" for yourself, as if you were the product...a very unique product. The universe is the customer. Our universe needs unique, individual products.

A sales presentation starts with an introduction, then goes into an explanation of the features and benefits of the product. So, learn the features and benefits of your product. On a piece of paper, write down all the unique characteristics of your product. Since you are the product, write down your physical features, your background, where you were raised, your schooling, your integrity, your principles and values, your skills, your innate talents. Put together your sales presentation as if it was the most important presentation in the world; as if just creating the presentation would give you the happiness and success you desire for the rest of your life.

For example, your features and benefits presentation may go something like this. Hello, my name is Susan. I am professional, reasonably attractive, and well spoken. Therefore, I can fit into most social situations relatively easily. I grew up in a small town with honest, hardworking citizens who taught me the value of a good day's work and the importance of handling all situations with integrity. You can count on me. My background includes not only formal schooling through high school, but a valued exposure to the corporate real world environment. These experiences enable me to offer positive contributions towards achievement of established goals. I have over-come specific challenges throughout my adult life that have made me stronger and more balanced in my approach to all situations, and so on...

When writing your features and benefits, go into as much detail as possible. And, remember, sell yourself on YOU. Stay on the positive side.

If a little voice in your head throws you an "objection" to your sales presentation, acknowledge the objection and get back to the positive. Explain the benefits of your unique version of the product. For example, if the little voice comments about your looks, saying "Susan, I like everything about you, but I think you are just a little too short. I need someone taller." Your response could be "I can appreciate what you are saying. Sometimes it's nice to have a taller version of this model. However, let me tell you why this model was designed to be shorter. There are many styles of clothing that look better on this version. With the proper presentation of dress and hairstyle, the shorter version is very distinctive. Many people feel that the compact version offers more flexibility. The ability to maneuver in small spaces can be beneficial as well, and of course, the smaller version is very huggable." It's beneficial to take the focus off external appearance and put it on your pure "specialness", your "huggability".

During this exercise, delight in yourself. It might feel awkward because you may not have allowed yourself this experience before, but choose to really treasure yourself. Don't just "like" yourself. I may like my smile, but I really *treasure* the way I glow! Choose to absolutely adore all those unique things about yourself. Really, really cherish everything about you. Be intimate with yourself. Try to use words that you can really feel.

Finally, finish your presentation with these words: "This particular model is unique. There is no other one available in the world. There has never been one like this in the past, and there will never be another like it in the future. This model belongs to me."

It is imperative that we respect ourselves. Recognize this truth: You are you, and you are the only you...therefore, you are special.

Once you have completed your "personal sales presentation", place it where you can read it REGULARLY. This reinforcement will remind you that you are a worthy individual. If you truly believe in yourself, then by many definitions you're already a success and deserve to be congratulated.

I discovered that once I had a spiritual belief and a belief in myself, I could now choose to believe that together, my Higher Power and I could set a direction for my life. And though I do not control all things in my life, these beliefs literally drive me down the path of success. They empower me. Upon reflection, I observe that even the smallest success is empowered by my belief that my God is with me and that I am capable and worthy of achievement. So these three fundamentals, (1) belief in a Power greater than yourself; (2) belief in yourself; and (3) belief that together, you can empower personal success, will allow you to experience personal peace and literally thrust you into a state of success that before, was unknown. This is the beginning.

Belief Maintenance

Belief requires maintenance. Remember, we are all constantly changing. If we allow it, others will change us or we will allow the circumstances to change us. We maintain our belief foundation by constantly affirming ourselves, reading through our personal sales presentation, and forgiving ourselves for our mistakes. Again, mistakes are a part of success. We need not be concerned. It's a learning experience. We flirt with serenity.

Though our beliefs can be instantly affected by whatever we feel at a given moment, we don't have to be afraid of our feelings. We can stay with them. We can manage our fear. They are our feelings and we are worthy of them. We can learn to establish eloquent communication with our inner selves that says we are capable, competent, loving, caring and worthy of being here, despite any circumstances.

When we have a strong belief foundation, it frees us to believe in possibilities. With that belief, we can achieve and we can accomplish. The strength to believe in ourselves gives us the right to believe that we can succeed...and that is flirting with serenity.

The following short poem has helped many come to believe in themselves and affirm their self-worth.

I am worthy

Not because of the car I drive
Not because of the clothes I wear
Not because of who I know
or where I live.

I am worthy

Not because I dig the deepest hole
Not because I climb the highest mountain
Not because of where I work
or what I do.

I am worthy

Not because my boss or friends say
Not because my parents or children say
Not because my mate says,
because He says.

I am worthy

Even when I don't feel it.
When I am alone,
or in a crowd,
When I am in love,
or not.

I am worthy

because I am true to myself.
From the day I was born
until forever
I am worthy just because...
I am.

And,
I am...
good enough.

3

Storms of Fear

Each of us has two forces, or energies, within. Like the Dark Side of the Force in *Star Wars*, these energies within us naturally strive for everyday dominance. As in nature, the negative self and positive self are involved in a never-ending civil war. Often, it is our unconscious choice to let the negative self win the battles. To flirt with serenity, we must consciously make an effort to let our positive self dominate. For many of us, if we don't consciously choose the positive self, the negative self will naturally dominate. Just does.

Let the Positive Win

We must learn to allow the positive self to win. One way to visualize this is to picture in your mind the negative you and the positive you, side by side. Then reduce the size and brightness of the negative picture. Make the positive you larger. In other words, take a mental picture of you in a depressed negative posture and one of you in a strong, positive posture. The negative you is a wallet size picture while the positive you is an 8 x 10. Keep the positive picture of you at the forefront of your conscious thought.

The positive self is the one that can make calculated choices that are good for us. Our positive self has an awareness. It can think about what is good for us, what we need. It's the self that can choose to no longer believe in those harmful or self-destructive behaviors that we learned from others. It can attract good things to us and sense what is best for us. Don't ignore it in favor of the negative self. Let your positive self win.

Fear Triggers

We often put roadblocks in front of our positive self because of fear. Uncontrolled fear can be one of the most negative emotions we can experience. In many cases, the basis of difficult-to-manage emotions, such as fear, is toxic shame. Toxic shame is a negative feeling about who we are that can completely extinguish our lifespark. That "less than" feeling is usually "given" to us by someone else, most often someone who is a primary caretaker. We take on their shame, even though it's not really about us. When we don't feel good about ourselves, we develop a defense system that can lead to extraordinary fear, anger, rage, manipulation and a long list of other uncomfortable emotions and behaviors. The renowned therapist and author, John Bradshaw, discusses toxic shame at length in his writings. To discuss these emotions therapeutically is beyond the scope of this book. However, since fear can often stand in the way of a flirtation with serenity, there is value in suggesting an understanding of it.

Healthy fear is okay. Healthy fear is that emotion that urges us to be cautious, prudent, practical, and pragmatic. Healthy fear is that smart awareness that tells us not to write another check because there isn't enough money left in the account to cover it. But when fear freezes us, it can be destructive, preventing us from making choices that lead to success and certainly interfering with our state of flow. Fear that immobilizes us causes intimidation and non-belief. This kind of fear keeps us from writing any check at all because we don't believe we can manage money and, if we do write a check, we will be broke and homeless. It can be stifling and smothering, and can result in extraordinary emotional imbalance.

Why We Fear

Fear is usually an emotional concern about an imagined event that triggers a negative response. Usually, our fear is about the future, but based on a past experience. We believe, or "project", that if certain events occur, we will be hurt or in danger. That belief is based on conditioning or "old messages" that we received in the past. Often, that conditioning was negative or abusive.

Contemporary therapist, Harville Hendrix, talks about the Old Brain and the New Brain. The Old Brain is made up of all our memories and learned behaviors. It only recalls past situations, behaviors and results. It takes old stuff, brings it into the present as real and expects us to behave or react the same way in the future. Old Brain thinking is very primitive and the urges and compulsions feel instinctual. Actually, the Old brain is brain-less. It doesn't think. That's why it's so dangerous. The New brain is a more conscious brain that is capable of thinking for itself. The New Brain is "new and improved". It can choose.

A popular acronym for fear is Future Events Appearing Real. And, that is what happens. Projections from our Old brains make the POSSIBILITY of harm seem real. And, if our negative self is dominant, we choose to make that our reality. Fear distorts the possibilities. It's a saboteur that tells you to expect the worst in any situation or circumstance, to doubt others and doubt yourself. It has been said that "fear is the darkroom where all our negatives are developed". It centers us in the future by recalling the past and keeping us from taking action today.

A universal reality is that not only can we not predict the experiences of the future, but it is apparent that NOTHING turns out EXACTLY like we had anticipated. Even if we anticipate a positive outcome, it is never exactly like we projected! It's the negative conditioning that dominates our thoughts resulting in our being "frozen" in place. So, how do we get "unstuck"? How do we move through fear?

Fear About Loss

Fear is about loss. We are afraid we will lose something or someone. And we fear that loss will make our life intolerable. Interestingly, this belief doesn't make sense if we've already begun to accept life's circumstances, that the winds of change are always blowing. It doesn't make sense if we flirt with serenity. In other words, though loss can be painful, sad, irritating, frustrating and whatever else, it does not make life intolerable if we accept that loss is part of the deal. Again, I don't mean to infer that we should be apathetic or unfeeling or anything that leads to denial or isolation. But, should we experience a painful loss, we can keep it in perspective and accept that it doesn't have to be our whole life. Life needn't be defined by its problems. Struggle is part of life, not life itself.

All our fears can be grouped into six "categories" of loss:

Loss of financial security
Loss of acceptance (not belonging)
Loss of health
Loss of youth
Loss of life
Loss of someone important (abandonment)

Though these are not in any particular order or hierarchy and there could be many sub-categories, many of our fears have their basis in fear of abandonment. Many people that have difficulty managing their lives have, as a motivational core, a fear of abandonment. If we lose our money, we will be abandoned. If we lose our health, we will be abandoned. If we grow old, we will be abandoned. If we don't look or act a certain way, we will be abandoned. If we don't handle this account perfectly, we will be fired (abandoned). And sadly, this is sometimes true. Some important people we care about may leave if we don't live up to their expectations. It's too bad and it's very sad. But as we mature and travel towards personal peace, we can strive to become secure enough with ourselves to let others choose not to be with us.

Living with the fear that we will be abandoned by those we care about will only cause anxiety and emotional imbalance. Life is going to happen. Perhaps, better choices can be made. "Maybe, they won't leave!" "I'm worthy even if they do leave!" "Maybe if I change, life will change!" Does it really make sense to center my life on fear? Can I really wink at success with my eyes closed?

I believe fear can be managed ... not eliminated ... but managed. I encourage you to feel your fear. If you don't acknowledge it, it stays with you. You can't begin to manage it if you deny it. What you resist, persists. Denying your fear, or any emotion, is what leads to frozen feelings, immobilization and getting stuck. The journey seems to stop.

Recipe for Managing Fear

Here is a proven recipe for managing fear and MOVING FORWARD.

1. Feel it. Acknowledge that you are afraid. It's okay to be afraid. Many of us were taught that it's not okay. We were taught this by our society, our culture and often a dominant parent. "It's not manly to be afraid." "Fear is a sign of weakness." These beliefs are wrong. While it may be inappropriate to act out your fears in a destructive way, it is okay to be afraid. It's okay to be really scared! So, be aware of your fear.

And, bring it up to your conscious. It's okay, you have a positive self that will help you manage it.

2. Ask yourself, "How afraid am I?" On a 1 to 10 scale, with 1 being mildly concerned and 10 being life threatening, how afraid am I? Your answer will help put your fear into perspective and often, surprise you. Also, notice what you are truly afraid of. Ask yourself "Am I afraid of something that may happen today or something that might happen in the future? How far in the future?" "Is it based on fact or phobia? Is it Old brain fear? Is it fear based on a past outcome?" "Was I a child when I last felt this fear? Can I handle it better as an adult?" All of these questions will help you get a handle on your fear and put it in the proper perspective relative to your life's journey and the coping tools available to you.

3. Now, after acknowledging your fear, simply tell your personal God, your Higher Power, your Supreme Spiritual Counselor. And, be aware that He is healing the false belief that created the fear, or preparing you to effectively handle your response to the real circumstances causing your fear. Fear is often described as the absence of faith. Conversely, allowing yourself to have fear is the ultimate in faith. Either way, your Higher Power is involved. So, through prayer or meditation or whatever personal method you use to speak with your God, begin to turn your fear over to a Power greater than yourself.

4. Thank your Higher Power for comforting you. Thank Him for the fear and the opportunity to grow.

Visualize His energy sharing in your fear. You can even visualize His taking the fear away from you. This may sound strange but by involving your Higher Power in this way, you are embracing your fear and faith at the same time. And, that leads to an acceptance of your circumstances. Acceptance of your circumstances leads to a mild flirtation with serenity. Isn't this great?

5. Write down all you know about your fear. This will likely take only a minute. By now, you have a pretty clear understanding of your fear and what is going on with it. Write down what you would have your Higher Power do with that fear. Write down what you will do the next time this fear comes around. THIS IS VERY IMPORTANT. The act of writing down your fear helps get it out. If you don't know where to start, start by writing "I am afraid!" and proceed to write down the answers to the questions you asked yourself in Step 2.

6. Tell someone else that you are afraid, how afraid and what you fear. This is often difficult for those of us who were conditioned to believe that we shouldn't express emotion or feelings. Particularly those feelings that might suggest weakness. But, doesn't the expression of fear really indicate strength? The telling of your fear actually suggests that you are aware and have, or are trying to get, a handle on it. There is no one that has ever lived that did not have fear. "Fearless" does not mean that a person is without fear. It means managing fear or moving forward despite your fear. Therefore, by sharing your

fear with someone, you are connecting yourself to humankind.

The person you tell about your fear should be a safe person, someone who will not minimize it or become abusive in any way. One safe method of sharing your fear is to tell the person up front that you are not necessarily looking for a solution or any feedback. You are sharing this because you are in the process of working through a problem. No more, no less.

Who can you tell? Most of us don't realize how many resources for sharing we have. A spouse, friend, minister, close co-worker, relative, therapist, counselor or support group are all good choices. If you are involved with a healthy 12-step support group, you are in one of the safest places in our world.

7. Finally, ask yourself this question: "What is one thing I would be doing if I didn't have this fear?" Then, do it once. That's right, just once.(Wink) Ultimately, you must take action. You are now in a position to act. You have all the support and strength you need to proceed. While you act, feel the fear diminishing, visualize the energy of your Higher Power sharing in the action. The fear now becomes a manageable emotion, not a "monster" that is undefined, uncontrolled and immobilizing.

What we've done here is tap into your positive self. Your self that can think and choose consciously. Your self that has a spiritual backbone and can choose to override old messages. We let that self win the war. By taking action just once, you begin to establish new conditioning. You have a new precedent. This new precedent has an association with action, growth, moving forward and living, rather than an association with pain, immobilization, aloneness and mere existence. Now your positive self can choose to do it again. It can practice managing the fear. It gets easier and easier. Do it once, again. And then, do it once again. Now you're getting a little flirtatious!

As you practice managing your fear, remember it's okay to be afraid. Everyone is. We all have crises and problems to overcome. But all things do pass, and we learn and grow from these happenings.

Beyond the Storm

Each of us has had and will have some very difficult times in our lives when we are full of fear. Fear that makes it difficult to see clearly that there will be healing, new opportunities, success and peace. I had one of these times when I experienced a business failure, financial trauma, divorce, loss of family, and a personal health crisis all within six months. During this time in my life, when I was full of fear and it seemed that there was no way out, a dear friend wrote:

> *Some may see a dreary storm. I see during and beyond... I see you as the large, strong ship. Some tears in the sails, but the most important parts still together...going to "make it" through this storm. No one can get out to help you through any part of it. It's*

too treacherous to get to you, you must do it on your own...and you will. When it is over...and doesn't this storm seem to be lasting forever?...you will look back and be so proud of yourself that you made it.

You are thinking that you had all the sailing techniques known to man, some from friends, many from family and many out of your own creation and special style - "but this storm makes me feel so scared and tired, I can't remember any of them". You will...when you let go to that power that is bigger than you...when you get outside of yourself, you will gather a greater understanding of things you already know, you will gather techniques that are important and leave others behind.

After the storm... you will lighten the boat for smoother sailing. You will not go where it is not wise for you to go. You will be prepared for all kinds of weather, and you will be able to "sense a storm" before it comes and ride through the surprise ones better, because you will remember "the big one(s) you did survive".

Storms don't last forever. You will make it through. You won't ever be able to convince anyone of how bad it was...they may say they know...they had been in storms themselves, but they weren't these...no one can know but you...and in time, you won't even need to try to tell them. You will be too busy repairing and preparing.

The bottom line is...you are constructed of the finest material, created with love and thought, cared for in the finest of ways. You have the right stuff to come out of this with grace and style and give even a greater meaning to the "art of sailing".

Your friend,
another sailor

Realize that there has never been an instance in history...in all time...when a storm was not followed by calm. It is a gracious law of Nature that calm follows the storm. Trauma is followed by peace.

Now that we are beginning to learn about managing our emotions, let's explore a way to apply these techniques to our own growth, our goals in life, our understanding of success.

4

Find Your Favorite Fire

Understanding Choice

Setting goals begins with recognizing the importance of choices. We can only set appropriate and challenging goals when we accept that we have all the choices in our life. It is absolutely and entirely up to us to choose the lifespace we want. Once we accept that we have choices, we can then acknowledge those things that turn us on, or light our fire. We can find our favorite fire!

We are the only ones that can put restrictions or limitations on our goals. That may seem unrealistic; that there are, in fact, many restrictions that life and society places on us. But, I would argue that there are numerous examples of people that have achieved incredible things under the most extreme circumstances, from the unlikely heroes in today's news, to historic figures such as Martin Luther King, Helen Keller and Picasso, to recognizable celebrities such as Michael Jackson and Itzak Pearlman. It didn't matter where they lived, what color they were, who their parents were, how much money they had, where they worked, or anything having to do with their circumstances.

These people knew they had choices. The only limitations were those they placed on themselves and, with respect to their talent and achievements, they chose not to place any. It is true that our world challenges us on this belief. There is evidence everywhere that says "you can't choose, you are stuck where you are." And, yes, there are occasional parameters given. But, we needn't confuse parameters with limitations. Parameters are simply the occasional boundaries that dictate appropriate behavior in a given situation, but they do not necessarily suggest limitations that prevent accomplishment.

My serenity is determined, to a great extent, by my ability to avoid letting the power in my circumstances affect my choices.

The only time we don't have a choice is when we're experiencing compulsive or obsessive behavior, or acting out an addiction. When a person is obsessed or experiencing addictive behavior, choosing becomes nearly impossible. These behaviors are a result of many things, including a subconscious effort to "medicate" our feelings. We "feel" we "have to" behave in certain ways. An active workaholic *must* work, an active over-eater *must* eat.

Despite these inclinations, with conscious awareness, we can choose not to be in our behavioral addictions. We can choose to come out of the denial that blindfolds awareness, elect to discover balance and recover from obsessive behavior. Despite all the old messages and circumstances that seem to send us in an obsessive direction, we can choose not to be a result of our past. The millions of people in recovery from addictions and obsessive behaviors are proof that we can choose.

We can choose to be what we choose to be.

Notwithstanding some health related afflictions, begin to accept that everything we do as an adult is a choice. Even if a gun is pointed at my head telling me to do something unpleasant or be shot, I have a choice. The prudent choice may be evident, but nevertheless, I do have a choice. When we can begin to realize that everything we do is a choice, we can begin to flow through life feeling a little more serenity. We can recognize that, in a very real sense, each of us has many alternate futures, and it is up to us to choose. Within this context, it has been said that the real purpose of time is to give us the opportunity to choose our future experiences, or how to interpret our past experiences.

Choosing Your Personal Lifespace

You can choose responsibility for your own direction and to dwell in your own lifespace. Your lifespace is the environment, the setting, the people, opportunities and behaviors you choose to include in your life. If you don't like your lifespace, you can choose to change it. Sometimes it will be difficult. But let's not confuse difficult with impossible. Go ahead and create a revised lifespace. When you create a new lifespace, you can then dwell in that place. If you choose, you can change and create still another lifespace. Be willing to choose to create your lifespace, dwell in it, change it and then continue that journey. Create, dwell, change; create, dwell, change,... and enjoy the process of those choices. The willingness to change remains. An old Zen Master stated that, in everyday life, it is undesirable to be attached to one's choices. You can choose but remain free to choose, and free in the result of your choice.

The point of this process is to recognize that ultimately, you will accept all the choices and eventually prioritize them. And, at a given point in time, your lifespace will depend on which "choice" is the highest priority at that time. There is no final destination. Enjoying the process of life is the ultimate success and the most joyous flirtation with serenity.

Goals, as part of your life and its inherent choices, can also change. After all, they are YOUR goals. So, why all this fuss about goals? Particularly when we are trying to flow through life. Because being in a State of Flow does not mean we are without direction. Once again, recognize that you will naturally strive for certain experiences in life. These experiences can be determined by you or by someone else.

Many of us have conducted our lives in a response to rules of "supposed to"... "live up to"... the "shoulds" and the "oughta's". If we don't choose to establish our goals, someone else will. We will be at the mercy of someone else's goals. Rather than being ourselves, we learn to adapt. Our adaptive self lives in response to the desires of others. We lose our real or authentic self in this effort. For the most part, everything we make happen is the result of our goals; everything that happens to us is the result of someone else's goals.

I didn't have any goals, so I became a victim of everyone else's goals.

We already know how to set goals. We already set them subconsciously. When we get up to walk across the room, our mind establishes the goal of getting to the other side of the room. Then our brain calculates exactly what action has to take place in order to achieve that goal and sets this action in motion. Though this is a simple goal and easy to achieve, it's evident that our brain does *know how* to do it. What we must learn to do is bring this process to a conscious level on a routine basis.

Setting goals is necessary to achieve success by almost any definition. Goals can be used to see specifically where you want to be, how you want to be, what you want to become. Also, there is evidence that, by some universal or mystical law, you can attract your goals to you. Setting goals is important so you have something specific to pull to you. When goals are used as benchmarks, they offer a measure of whether you are going in the direction you choose with your life.

Growth Goals

What about those necessary tasks that are simply not attractive or pleasant to pursue? Things like that unpleasant paperwork that "has" to get done, or that long commute to the office, or the "work" of allowing a good friend the opportunity to fall in love with the "wrong" person. These goals are reframed into part of a larger picture. They become part of a larger goal, a stepping stone. These pursuits are a combination of a goal and a growth opportunity - a "Groal", if you will. Perhaps we can use the word Groals to describe those goals that offer growth experiences during our journey to success. Even if we don't always get exactly what we had hoped for (remember the twists and turns), we are still growing and learning.

When setting goals, we can allow that goals are not destinations, but rather benchmarks. A place towards which we can grow. It's important to know that goals are most effective when they are personal and subject to change, and when there is always a "next" one. Those that have achieved their goals also agree that goals should be written down on paper. This makes them more real and allows us to focus on them more readily. Again, goals are predetermined, but flexible. Having said that, please don't interpret "flexibility" as an opportunity to be wishy-washy. Goals change only when we discover upon reflection that we are no longer interested in that particular goal or it is no longer consistent with our values or needs, NOT WHEN WE ARE TIRED OR FEEL THAT WE MIGHT NOT ACHIEVE THE GOAL. For example, you may have set a goal of becoming Vice President of your company. Upon discovering that it required you to relocate with your family to a less than desirable part of the country with poor schools and high crime, you chose to relinquish that goal and set a new one that allowed you to continue with the lifestyle you most desire; not because you couldn't, or weren't capable, of becoming a vice president.

Boundaries Before Goals

Before we can set the typical achievement, or accomplishment-oriented goals, we first take a good look at our principles and values, define parameters in which we will accomplish our goals, and set boundaries on our behavior and that of others. In other words, we must first determine what our value-oriented goals are in relation to what we want out of life...the settings, opinions, desires and beliefs on which we will not compromise...the principles we will honor under any circumstance. Principles and values are the essence of being human, of being significant and a universal part of the whole. If our goals are not in harmony with what we truly want life to be, it will be virtually impossible to achieve success with serenity.

A Foundation of Principle

Since your principle-oriented goals will be the foundation for all others, it's wise to take time to truly evaluate how you want life to be for you. Again, this is personal. Yet, it seems the most desirable principles allow you to feel a part of us all. To give an example of some principle-oriented goals that govern all others, here is a synopsis of goals developed early on in my journey.

1. Have peace of mind.

2. Live a long, physically and mentally whole, happy, spiritually balanced life.

3. Sustain an emotionally healthy, reliable relationship with my life mate.

4. Have safe, dependable relationships with family and friends.

5. Have financial security and contentment.

6. Make a positive contribution to humanity.

7. Have fun.

Before developing the philosophy for *Wink at Success, Flirt with Serenity*, my goals were not based on a foundation of principle. Primarily, they were based on acquiring and achieving. While there is nothing wrong with these things when kept in perspective, they did not represent anything of a spiritual substance to me, and therefore, I stayed "busy" doing things that kept me separate from myself, those around me and my spirituality.

My principle-oriented goals represent an understanding I have with myself. All other goals fall within this overall setting. I will not choose to do things that will compromise my lifelong goal of having peace of mind. This governs my honesty, integrity and belief system. Further, I will not establish relationships that are not safe and reliable. And my actions must be prudent, reflecting financial responsibility. Though every moment will not reflect enjoyment, I strive to include fun and celebration in my daily life. And so on.

The wonderful thing about a principled foundation is that it does not require reaction. The principles are constant and consistent. They don't change. They don't need approval or validation from anyone or anything outside. Therefore, they are stronger than any circumstance.

Because we're human and sometimes respond to those old scripts, we sometimes choose actions contrary to our principles. It's okay; we soon learn that when we choose to act against our principles, the outcome is usually negative. When we act in harmony with our personal principles, we empower ourselves toward a desirable outcome.

Interestingly, honoring our principles can sometimes feel like we're betraying someone else. So to keep from betraying someone else, we just give up on ourselves and our principles. Once again, it's wise to avoid "others" thinking and embrace "self" thinking.

Permission to Achieve

Once we have established our principles and governing goals, we can establish achievement-oriented goals. There are many books and sources telling us how to do this, some listed at the end of this book. There are several areas worth examining. These include health and physical matters, economic goals, and lifestyle or "thing" goals. We can allow ourselves to dream and establish goals that will stretch us. It's okay to have everything we want as long as what we want does not compromise our personal values and does not harm others. We are deserving and worthy of everything good in life. Wink at success means giving ourselves permission to have.

By the way, as you make choices, set goals and generally create your life, consider that it's okay to be unique or a bit eccentric. If you think of anyone who's "successful", notice that when put in the proper context, that person can be considered eccentric. For example, Ben Franklin, Ghandi, Marlon Brando, Mohammad Ali, Madonna, Albert Einstein, Picasso, Lee Iaccoca, John Lennon, Elizabeth Taylor, and the list goes on. You get the point. So, if it pleases you and doesn't hurt or limit anyone else, you can give yourself permission to be eccentric. But, also remind yourself to avoid becoming obsessively eccentric! Working until nine o'clock EVERY night does not constitute "a little eccentricity"!

Goal Guides

When establishing goals, there are a few more "guides" worth reviewing. First, we make our private life more important than our public life. That is, we establish goals that will keep us pleased with our inner selves, goals that will enhance our personal life with family, friends and God.

Upon self-examination, I was amazed at how often my motivation for doing something was so others would acknowledge me, think of me or stroke me in some way. People that establish ego-driven goals based on public recognition often find themselves obsessed and driven for shallow, unfulfilling, ultimately meaningless goals. This happens because there doesn't exist a strong foundation based on principles for these goals. They are driven by the ego, the desire for outside recognition rather than the desire to contribute. While a healthy ego is necessary to motivate one to achieve, my experience is that a goal based solely on ego fulfillment limited my quest for serenity and separated me from others.

Follow Your Bliss, Blissfully

Examining our motivations or inspirations can help us establish worthwhile goals. It seems best to pay less attention to the THINGS that motivate us, placing more focus on the ACTIVITIES and FEELINGS that inspire us. For example, if you enjoy the activity associated with tinkering in the garage, consider a goal based on that activity such as inventing a new or improved tool. Or, if your interest is music, it might be fun to consider collecting old records, writing songs or setting up a home recording studio. Center your goals on these aspirations. Follow your bliss, blissfully! Find your favorite fire! Observe that when we are doing exactly what we want to do, nothing else seems to matter at that moment. We can consciously pursue those activities instead of doing them by accident. I learned a great deal from Sharon, who, when asked about her activities, consistently responded "Because this is what I want to do." She never felt the need to explain or seek approval for her bliss. The stuff that inspires our senses will generate goals and desires that allow us not only to wink at success and achievement, but flirt with serenity along the way.

Ego-based Goals

The acquisition or control of property can be the result of honorable inspiration IF it is based on contribution. For example, to build something that will contribute to the economy or society, or to create jobs, is a worthwhile aspiration. But when the control of property is the inspiration unto itself (a monument to the "owner"), it is ego-based and usually disastrous. One need only to observe the rise and fall of Donald Trump to witness a good example of what can happen when the property becomes bigger than the contribution. I created my own little version of this story by thinking that having a big, expensive house would make me feel important and "up with the Joneses". Big, expensive houses are okay, but not when its acquisition distorts or sabotages all other opportunities. Therefore, I find that acquisition is rewarding only as a by-product or natural result of creating, giving, producing or serving.

The acquisition or control of people is an unhealthy inspiration simply because the real control of other people is virtually impossible. It smothers the lifespark in each of us and goes against any universal spirituality that brings us together. When we attempt to control others, they ultimately leave, literally or emotionally, to escape. They feel it's their only choice. Employees feel they work for a dictator. Friends feel they are being manipulated. Romantic relationships dissolve because one is deprived of personal identity. Even whole governments based on the control or limiting of human rights have fallen apart. All of us have an intense spiritual need to feel valued for ourselves.

A good self-monitoring exercise is to develop a line of questioning for yourself that will help determine your motives. Use the words "I WANT... SO THAT...". If your answer to the "So that..." part results in the manipulation or control of another person's lifespark, it's not likely an appropriate motivation.

The achievement of that goal will not lead to peace of mind. Rather than winking at success and flirting with serenity, you may be courting failure and embracing inner conflict.

All There Is About Money

There is something we can accept about money as a goal. It can be intoxicating. Money is often used as a measure of success as in the case of those "most wealthy" or "richest in..." surveys that turn up regularly in popular magazines. While the amount of money a person accumulates may measure the success of a business venture or investment strategy, it does not necessarily reflect a person's success in life.

Money itself is merely a means of exchange, a currency. Money is good when it is earned and received as the result of creating, giving, producing or serving. However, the accumulation of money is not a worthy goal unto itself. Though once the accumulation of money was a primary motivation for me, I've since learned that many people who have achieved financial fortune did not start out just to accumulate large sums of money. Rather, the accumulation of money was the natural outcome of creating, giving, producing or serving. Because they are not based on contribution, ego-driven goals centered on money usually create conflict, imbalance and obsession rather than peace of mind. Overwhelmingly, the statistics show that most of those who merely inherit or "come into" financial wealth without a genuine contribution, do not have the capability of keeping it. We can only assume that they don't have the proper foundation to cope with their "success". Simply, to have money without contribution is not a goal that automatically creates long term success and serenity.

This concept, however, does not imply that we should not desire wealth. On the contrary, money does help create choices, particularly those having to do with quality of life. The ambitious, honorable desire to create financial wealth is okay. Having money or attaining financial wealth is often made to be complex. Many sophisticated wealth building formulas are available and each of us can choose to create the circumstances that lead to income opportunities. However, the amount of income is usually not as critical as the management of the income. I agree with financial experts who say real wealth is not how much money you make, but how much is left over.

To embrace the philosophy of winking at success, one simply needs to know that it is wise to spend less money than you take in. As easy as it sounds, there are those that find the spending of money an obsessive trap that greatly compromises serenity. I had to come to terms with confusing messages about money management. At times, I would get stuck. When I didn't have much money, I wouldn't spend any 'cause I was waiting until I had some; and when I did have money, I wouldn't spend any 'cause if I did, I was afraid I wouldn't have any. A vicious circle that led to an immobilizing fear of my financial circumstances and did not permit me or my family to enjoy life. This kind of immobilization and emotional confusion led to compulsive or "explosive" spending behaviors. As a result, I sometimes spent carelessly just to make myself feel good.

If the appropriate spending of money is difficult for you, recognize that anything over basic needs is a gift to yourself. We all deserve gifts and we should treat ourselves when we can, but recognize the expenditure as a gift or treat. Gary, a peaceful acquaintance of mine, determined that the only material things "needed" were shelter, a bed, a chair, a reliable mode of transportation, food, basic clothing, a pair of shoes, a pair of glasses, available medical care and a book to read. Upon establishing his "needs", he was then able to provide himself and family with a perspective that said anything beyond those needs was a gift. He is wealthy, comfortable and living with an enviable gratitude for the many gifts this viewpoint brings to him each day. When it comes to the appropriate spending of money, a better example of flirting with serenity would be difficult to find.

Successful money management requires pragmatic planning and the calculated expenditure of reasonable sums to meet your personal needs. Your planning can even include "spontaneous" expenditures. A sensible guide is to save at least ten percent of all you earn, spend twenty percent on reducing past debts, thereby allowing you to live on seventy percent of all you earn. This may sound simplistic, but these are principles that will get you started and contribute to your flirtation with serenity.

Relationship Goals

One of the most helpful suggestions I ever received was to set goals for the relationships in my life. We can set goals on how we want our relationships to be with our marital partner, family, friends, associates and superiors. We can determine how we want the relationship to be with regards to proximity, communication, responsibilities and obligations. Sometimes, we may be able to establish these goals together with the other person. For example, when setting marriage goals, it makes sense to share your goals and expected roles in the areas of career, household chores, house cleaning, decorating, repairs, cooking, style of home, how to spend holidays and vacations, leisure time, sex, money and investments, children, relatives, friends, health issues, support, nurturing and expected communication. So many marriages are disappointing because the two never get together to discuss how they want things to be, how they want to harmonize or what they expect from the relationship and life in general, not just what they want to accomplish or have.

Recognizing it is not healthy or possible to control someone else, some relationships may require you to establish your goals individually and just manage your own behavior within that relationship. At least you will have set boundaries and be able to continue your personal flirtation with serenity.

Optimum Excellence

These are YOUR goals. Compare only to your personal goals, not to other people's accomplishments. This is your life. Run your own race, choose your own setting. It's not a contest with anyone or anything else.

I have found it helpful to avoid striving for absolute perfection in achieving my goals. When I push for perfection, I only make myself and those around me miserable. However, I can flirt with serenity by striving for "optimum excellence". The key word being optimum. This viewpoint suggests that all things considered and given imperfect people, places and things, this is the best I can do at this given moment. Optimum excellence is something that I and others can live with. Once I feel I've achieved optimum excellence, I can let go. It's enough! By now, I have a full-fledged affair with serenity!

There is no perfection,
but the journey...
the wonder of the journey.

Passion vs. Obsession

The concepts outlined in this book are about Calculated Life Management, not compulsive control. Many people set goals, then go about pursuing those goals with a "burning desire", an obsession. To flirt with serenity, we pursue our goals with all the energy we have, but MAINTAIN A HEALTHY PASSION FOR OUR GOAL, NOT AN OBSESSION. What's the difference? If you put your heart into it, it's passion. If you put your soul into it, it's obsession. Obsession is not healthy. People with obsessive behaviors lose themselves. They lose their balance, they lose touch with reality and they separate from their soul. Your soul is your connection to a higher Power and to the universe. It is your spiritual umbilical cord to all things greater, the connection that makes us one. And it is your spiritual bond with your treasured self. If you give up your soul, you actually become separate from all others. The dichotomy is that when you are passionate, yet detached, your individuality and your specialness can stay connected. Magically, you remain a part of all of us.

Once goals are established, the tough part for most people is to take action towards the fulfillment of those predetermined goals. Action should be viewed as the next logical step. It's just follow up, the application of our vision. There has never been a hard-to-understand solution for getting started. It's just something we do. The difficulty is that many of us have those old messages running around in our heads that tell us we can't. Or, we are simply afraid that the results will not be what we want. That's what this book is about, getting through the roadblocks, deciding it's okay to have learning experiences. It's okay to be imperfect. We believe in, and trust ourselves. We do it once. We have the energy. Take that little step toward your favorite fire. Then keep trying, with passion. Keep at it until you get what you want.

If you can't figure out where to start, or where the beginning is - you are there. Start where you are. If you can't figure out when to start - the time is now. Now is a good time. Wink at success. Then follow up with sustained action. Perhaps only a single action each day, sustained over many days. Persistence towards your goals. You can be very close to your favorite fire and not know it. You can be five feet from the edge of the forest, and still be in the forest. So keep striving. You are capable of knowing how far to go. Leonardo DaVinci once said, "Oh Lord, thou givest everything at the price of an effort". Life is a series of efforts.

Winking at success is not about a driving force that generates complete and utter devotion to a cause, it's about a passion for life. A passion for goals that you have chosen, and it's best when you can achieve your goals while flirting with serenity, striving for peace of mind...and balance.

5

Quest for the Gray

In reviewing the concept of balance in our lives, it quickly becomes apparent that we are attempting to tackle a very, very difficult subject. There is little contemporary, self-help literature that does more than reference the concept of balance. "Everything in moderation" seems to be the dictum, but little is mentioned about what that really means or how to do it.

Finding balance is like trying to catch a bubble. Even if you see it, it's hard to grasp without "losing" it. With this awareness, we begin the process of discovering and sustaining balance.

The pursuit of any singular object, person or experience and the ignoring or denial of others causes imbalance. This one-sided dedication results in the loss of ourselves to something incomplete. For example, complete dedication to our work or a particular job leaves us with little on the side of fun, leisure, relationships or social endeavors. A definition of success ideally includes not only a conscious dedication to hard work but a time to sing.

The See-Saw

Finding and sustaining balance is the ultimate adventure, an ever changing treasure hunt. A most elusive concept, it's like trying to find the middle of a see-saw when we cannot see either end of the see-saw. The ends of the see-saw represent the extremes, and everyone has a different see-saw. How far should we go? The answer may be to go as far as we feel necessary without ignoring other people and experiences. As long as we give weight to the other side of the see-saw, we can maintain some balance. Only when we are singular or absolute in our pursuits do we lose our balance and hit the ground.

To maintain balance in our lives requires a very conscious and constant effort. We seek the middle ground, sense the optimum...quest for the gray. Finding the middle ground is actually a search for higher ground. In making a choice other than the extreme, we seek to identify a third choice, or alternative, that does not seem to be readily apparent. This effort actually carries us to a higher level of success in our relationships with ourselves and others. We discover a viewpoint that allows the extremes or differences to meet somewhere near the middle where a higher level of achievement and subsequent peace can occur.

No More Black and White

We are often taught that there is always a best answer. "Always" and "best" are absolute concepts generally subject to an individual judgement and therefore, really hard to achieve. We as individuals, groups and even whole nations seem to go to extremes in search of the ideal. This "absolute" notion is what destroys our opportunity for serenity. There is very little in our world that is absolute. There are seldom situations that are clearly black and white, there is usually gray. It's not all or nothing, either/or. Life isn't "always" good or bad, it's good AND bad.

*Another fortune cookie:
It is sometimes better to idealize the real
than to realize the ideal.*

Striving for balance in our lives is necessary, although in the practical sense, difficult to maintain. Conscious diligence is required to keep from going too far to one side or the other. If we give ourselves to our work, we ignore leisure. If we are singularly dedicated to leisure activities, our income producing activities suffer. We can choose to develop a conscious awareness of our daily thoughts and activities. An awareness that sets off a mental alarm when we're trying to find an *absolute* answer to a subjective situation, or find *the* answer when there are many answers, some of which would be acceptable and allow us to get on with our life.

And yet, there's a catch. If we don't commit ourselves to certain experiences, we will wind up accomplishing nothing. Without commitment, it's difficult to complete anything. So maintaining balance does not mean a lack of dedication to a person or experience. It just means that when we are striving to achieve, there is a CONSCIOUS AWARENESS that monitors our dedication, that knows when we are not at peace.

Remember that passion for a thing is very different from obsession. There is no harm in wanting to accomplish, only in being blindly driven to accomplish.

Enmeshment vs. Detachment

A singular dedication to a person or experience is called enmeshment. It means that I am allowing myself to become that experience, that the consequences of that experience are affecting my whole being. On occasion, you may have observed someone that got "too wrapped up" in a situation. They may have had an all-consuming, subconscious focus on spouse or family, work, money, drugs, possessions, church, friends, love or sex. This is a sign that they are leaning too far to one side and losing themselves in that experience. When this occurs, one can lose objectivity and the ability to maintain boundaries and make rational decisions. It's what happens when a person becomes addicted.

Addiction or obsession feels like "I won't be okay without...." In our subconscious, we feel "crazy" or "unmanageable" without the object of our obsession, whether it be another person, food, drugs, sex, work, shopping, etc. Instead of conscious awareness, there is a compulsive and all-consuming effort to have that experience. When in that unbalanced state, it's virtually impossible to consider choices or the consequences of behavior. Flirting with serenity becomes incomprehensible. With serenity, going to the extreme is the exception, rather than the rule.

Flirting with serenity is very much about detachment...the other side of enmeshment. There is little in life to teach us detachment and is usually only understood by studying concepts of "higher consciousness". In simple terms, detachment is the ability to view a situation without extreme emotion or involvement. It's like stepping away from the situation and viewing it from a distant corner of the room. The view includes looking at your own actions and behavior within that situation, much like watching a movie. Detachment doesn't mean we don't care or aren't willing to participate. It just means we can "see" the possibilities, alternatives and consequences without getting "too wrapped up". We don't get involved in the absolutes and can maintain a sensibility, a balance, a serenity.

Those that achieve detachment do not get too involved in "the problem". There is recognition that they cannot control other people, places and things. The success or failure - the outcome of a particular happening - is not necessarily about them and will not be a reflection of their capability or worthiness. Adopting that position really opens the door to freedom and a healthy passion for the experience. A passion that will not cause the see-saw to tip too far one way or the other, but rather contribute to the desired outcome of the experience.

When I become aware that I'm getting too wrapped up in a specific experience and I'm in "overwhelm" or going "crazy", it's time to Stop. Sit down. Be calm. I ask myself, "Is the outcome of this circumstance going to change my life? How much? Will it really matter tomorrow? In two weeks? In two years? Will I be able to continue my life pretty much as I want? Will I still have choices?"

If the answers to these questions make me feel trapped, I'm probably enmeshed. There are very few situations where a balanced person cannot, upon reflection and with awareness, put a situation in perspective and recognize their choices.

So how do we strive for balance? How do we maintain peace when the only thing we know is extremism? In summary, we start by having a conscious awareness that we must keep our mind's eye open to the middle ground, the quest for the gray. If we allow it, our spiritual guide will assist us. Also, during those moments when everything around us seems to be in conflict, or when we're becoming a little "crazy" trying to accomplish something - we practice detachment. We pause, step back and reflect. Removing ourselves from the picture of craziness usually leads to quick relief. Often, when I disentangle myself from a situation, it becomes easier to resolve. I can avoid impulsive decisions and give myself time to calculate a constructive action.

Going to RIO

Some of us have grown up feeling that we always have to be doing something. This belief keeps us unbalanced because we are obsessed with activity. You may know people whose primary daily motivation is to "go and do". They fill up their lives with activities or participations. Being calm, taking it easy or just spending time with themselves feels "empty" or "wierd". When we are "always busy" or "in everyone's business", we become a Human Doing, instead of a Human Being.

With respect for the process of life, I choose to believe we are each a Human Becoming...implying process and a universal spirituality. We can maintain humility and acknowledge that everything we do doesn't always matter, and therefore release ourselves from compulsive activity. Sometimes, we choose not to do anything. Sometimes, there really is nothing we can do. We just ride it out. I call this "going to RIO" (Ride It Out). Everything that goes on around me is not necessarily a comment on my life. I can see that I am PART of the plan, not THE plan. And, I can fill up the "empty" feeling with relaxation and joy.

The Only Moment That Counts

Balance also means staying in the present and leaving the past where it is. Many behaviors that cause enmeshment and imbalance are a reaction to old scripting from the past. Just because someone once said "you'll never amount to anything, unless..." doesn't mean you'll never amount to anything. Leave past experiences in the past. This is the only moment that counts. We can examine the past for knowledge and learning, but the past is not going on now. We can face past regrets and examine them for learning, but there is no need to indulge them. Learning from the past means an ever-lighter load of regrets. We tip our hat to the past and move on to live in the only time we can - the present.

Though planning and calculating your actions for the future is prudent, and having dreams is okay, it's not productive to "live" in the future. Many of us are so completely caught up in trying to anticipate every action, conversation and happening for the future we totally miss the opportunities of today. While contemplating the consequences of our actions and being aware of possible outcomes is prudent, "living" in each outcome only causes the breakup of our serenity. Constantly bringing the future into daily life will cause loss of balance, constant obsession and a loss of perspective.

We sabotage our success and serenity when we hold the past or the future too precious. Even though we can return to "HERE", we cannot return to "NOW". Therefore only the "NOW" need be held precious. This really is the only moment that counts. Living "one day at a time" or "taking it as it comes" are philosophies that are a necessary foundation for serenity.

Self Sabotage

If we're involved or enmeshed in an experience that is not going to directly impact our life, but will possibly impact someone else's, we detach...with kindness. We let them have their own chance for an outcome. Everyone deserves the opportunity to experience their own outcome, whether it be a success or learning experience. Getting involved when it's not our "stuff" is sabotaging our own success.

At times when we become aware that blaming others is non-productive and that we may be sabotaging ourselves, it's helpful to ask if our own thoughts, actions or projections are causing things to go in an undesirable direction. Sometimes our viewpoint can throw us out of balance and we sabotage our personal success. If this happens, we may have lost consciousness regarding our principles and values and self-examination may be in order.

Steven Berglas, a Harvard Medical School psychologist specializing in the treatment of successful people, says that those who "suffer" from success have avoided self-examination and have three or more of the four A's - Arrogance, a sense of Aloneness, the need to seek Adventure, and Adultery. Those that come crashing down from success have, in essence, imploded, or experienced profound self-sabotage. If we are to "own" success and serenity, we must be willing to develop a strong foundation that can withstand self-examination in light of these basic, but destructive, characteristics.

At the same time, on the other end of the see-saw, we are gentle with ourselves. Can your perception of yourself change the way things look? Are you making it worse than it is? Are you beating yourself up needlessly, just because you are human and you did a human thing? Can you forgive? Can you learn from what is going on around you? Being kind and understanding with ourselves can bring peace. When we recognize our own foibles, we can gently correct our course and move on.

The Victim Role

When coming from an unbalanced position, there are two questions we can ask ourselves about an experience that will almost certainly cause more imbalance and lead to obsession. Those questions are "How come?" and "Why?" Particularly, if it involves trying to determine WHY someone did this or HOW COME it went that way. Usually, these questions are asked while we are acting out the role of "victim". When in this state of mind, we are already out of balance and trap ourselves trying to "prove" that we are helpless. Often, the variables and personalities in a situation are so complex that we find ourselves searching obsessively for the answer to "How come?" Again, obsessive behavior isn't healthy. We can choose to be free.

The odds for personal success improve greatly when we ask "Why" or "How Come" from an empowering state of mind. In other words, ask "Why do I behave this way under these circumstances?" or "Now that this has happened, what can I do to take advantage of the circumstances?" or "What have I learned from this that can contribute to my success in the future?" or "How come this happens to me every time?" Truly, to wink at success, we must ask empowering questions...questions that empower us to examine circumstances and behaviors in a way that opens our minds for self-examination and allows us to receive the success and serenity we desire.

Forgiveness

Forgiveness helps us keep balance in our lives. We lose our balance when we do not forgive because it keeps us tilted toward negative emotions and separates us from others and ourselves. When we harbor ill feelings, we remain in our anger, disconnected from genuine experience. Forgiving reconnects us to others, and returns us to universal peace.

When we hesitate to forgive, it might be that we genuinely don't like what happened. Forgiveness doesn't mean we have to excuse or approve or endorse someone's behavior. Many of the wounds we suffer in our daily lives are simply abusive and not okay. But, accepting that these abusive behaviors are not about us and often come from those acting out their own troubled patterns ("victims of victims") does, at least, give us the opportunity to choose to let go of the anger or negative feelings toward that person just enough to get on with life. Forgiveness is an offspring of acceptance, because it is about giving up the fantasy that we can have a better past.

Most importantly, we can learn to forgive ourselves. Many of us spend an enormous amount of time beating ourselves up over the smallest things. It's okay to give ourselves a break. We can make mistakes, have negative emotions, misjudge an outcome. All of these things happen to everyone. We're all human. We seem to allow all kinds of strange happenings to occur with other people, governments, society, etc. We shrug it off with a reluctant acceptance that those things are just part of life. We can be just as accepting when we have something in our life that seems a bit exceptional. We're still okay. We can be gentle with ourselves.

In an effort to heal myself, I'll acknowledge that I feel like I've earned a black belt in self-loathing. I'm capable of making a small thing big, mentally beating myself to a pulp, and I have great difficulty forgiving myself for my character defects. During those times, its wise for me to simply "lighten up", reflect on my foundation, examine my motivations, acknowledge my human-ness, get centered on what I can do today and flow towards success.

We can respect ourselves, forgive ourselves and give serenity a big hug.

Time for You

The task of maintaining balance requires taking time for ourselves. Whether we meditate, reflect, pray, contemplate or whatever, we can take time to check our awareness, to check our reality and acknowledge our thoughts and feelings. Denying what is going on within us results in stuffed emotions that cause reactions leading to a loss of balance.

If we get too tied up in things outside us, we may not take time to untie the knots inside ourselves. We can't maintain balance while absorbing someone else's emotions and not acknowledging ours. It's like lying to ourselves. When we deny ourselves, anger sets in and we cross boundaries. We may not effectively communicate our ideas and cause even more unrest. On the other hand, when we are comfortable with our reality, we can respect others and contribute successfully to each endeavor.

Though flirting with serenity requires a certain flexibility and adaptability, it doesn't require that we become something other than ourselves. By practicing authenticity, we allow ourselves to feel our feelings and, when appropriate, put them into action. A good way to monitor authenticity is to occasionally stop, think about what you're thinking about, question your motivation and listen to yourself. Reflect on your principles and follow your spiritual guide.

Our Part in the Whole

We sometimes lose our balance when we are not conscious of our part in the whole. We are all on the same planet. At this writing, there is nowhere else to go. So, the choice to respect others seems to be one that's practical. If I may fearlessly climb onto my soapbox, I encourage you to care about children, nature, animals, and the environment. Even if you choose not to be active in those concerns, you can be caring and gentle. Have a reverence for life, respect vulnerability. There are people and other living things that do not hold up well because a temporary situation, such as homelessness, leaves them vulnerable. Our environment is vulnerable. Our children are certainly vulnerable. We can choose to respect boundaries, and allow those who are vulnerable to thrive and grow. In this way, we remain connected to the whole of our world. In being a respectful part, we flirt with serenity.

We Already Know How

Here are some reminders of what you already know:

Eat reasonably.
Exercise regularly.
Have fun. Seek adventure.
Make all you can.
Save all you can.
Give all you can.
Enjoy all you can.
Choose love.

All these things are fundamental to balance. Generally, I believe we already know this. We even know how. With only a few cultural exceptions, most of us *know how* to eat reasonably. We know to limit our intake of fat and cholesterol. We know we should eat substantial amounts of fruits, vegetables and other water-rich foods. We *know* we need to exercise regularly. We know that means exercise approximately thirty minutes a day or three hours a week. We know that aerobic exercise strengthens our cardiovascular system.

We *know how* to have fun. We know that it's fun to see a movie, go on a picnic, drink in a sunset, play games, fly a kite, search for perfect rainbows or take a vacation. We *know how* or can easily learn the basics of money management. Some days are for making a buck, some days are for saving a buck, some days are for managing a buck, some days are for enjoying a buck. And, we *know how* to choose love. We know that choosing to love means rejoicing in someone else as they are, respecting their choices, and willingly nurturing their being.

Without oversimplifying, the point is the basics are simple and if we want to learn more about any of these areas, the literature, guidance and experiences are readily available. It would be redundant to do more than suggest that we capitalize on what we already know as part of our quest for balance. Even though you may feel like you've forgotten, you *know how* to do it. To paraphrase a popular song, Oz didn't give anything to anyone they didn't already have.

Balance does not mean standing still in one place, in the middle of the see-saw. Balance isn't static. We may not always see the ends of the see-saw and therefore, not be able to calculate exactly where to stand, but we are aware of the extremes and consciously move back and forth to accommodate a balance, maintaining self-awareness about where we are at this moment. So, in life, balance is eternal, rather than static. This is particularly apparent during periods of growth. Again, Nature serves as an example of eternal balance. Though there are one hundred degree days and below freezing days, there is eternal movement back and forth between these extremes. For us, perhaps the key is to be aware of the hundred degree day and not stand outside until we collapse from the heat.

To quest for the gray is to maintain a vigilant, but gentle search for middle ground. An "everyday consciousness" that we don't have to go to extremes. We keep the focus on this moment and this place. If we become enmeshed with an experience, person or thing, chances are that we have some trapped feelings or we are trying desperately to heal an old emotional wound. Many of us begin the cycle of extremism when we do not acknowledge our true feelings, or unconsciously act out learned behaviors from the past that are not necessarily valid today. If we don't acknowledge or "claim" these feelings, we are subject to behaviors that "medicate" our feelings. Be aware. Extraordinary courage is required to ask yourself "Why am I reaching for this extra bag of potato chips?" or "Am I working late because I don't want to be somewhere else?" It takes extraordinary courage to honestly question our motivations. A great deal of effort is necessary to become intimate with ourselves, notice the imbalance...and quest for the gray.

6

Theme for Life

As preparation for this chapter began, life coincidentally presented me with still more opportunities to test the concepts suggested herein. Once again, confirmation that the process of life is ever changing, requiring continued effort to meet its challenges. Since life is seldom routine or predictable, it does not so much require rules for living, but rather the development of a theme. A theme for living suggests that life flows through broad, flexible concepts grounded in solid values, universal laws and natural growth; those concepts that put the odds in our favor for the successful achievement of our goals and the personal peace that comes with serenity.

The Willingness

As we move toward achievement in a particular endeavor, certain primitive, compulsive behaviors are occasionally triggered in each of us that can sabotage our efforts and allow serenity to elude our mind's grasp. So, first and always, it becomes necessary that we have the willingness to adopt this life of Success and Serenity. Though it's sometimes emotionally painful to discover how our behaviors stand in the way of success and personal peace, we recognize that there is often "profit" from the pain. Profitable pain is a teacher that says here is the opportunity to learn and grow so you can get on with living. We develop the desire to learn with newfound awareness, with our New brain. This means letting go of the Old brain scripts. When feeling "stuck", I consciously ask myself if there is something I need to let go of, or release. It may be a belief or expectation that will be emotionally disruptive to release, but ultimately beneficial and liberating. Letting go, I can move on with my journey.

In some instances, it's not so much an effort of will power to overcome the old triggers or behaviors, but reprogramming the triggers themselves. We learn to unlearn. We confront ourselves and allow the pain to teach us what hasn't worked, and we discover what will work. We are willing to take the steps, however difficult initially, that will bring personal success whether it involves career, family, finances, relationships, or spiritual pursuits.

Sometimes, we just have to be willing to be willing.

Experience tells us that we must be willing to do the hard stuff - willing to learn new ways, willing to participate, willing to be involved. That is, we cannot do it all by ourselves. Success involves relationships; relationships with ourselves, our God, family, spouse, children, bosses, associates, employees, friends, advisors, customers, suppliers, etc. Since having a successful life most likely will involve relationships with others, our theme for success can include a willingness to communicate effectively with others. Unfortunately, few of us have ever been exposed to enlightened, genuine communication. As a result, we communicate without listening, without saying what we mean, with manipulative or accusatory language and without a real desire to understand and be understood. The development of appropriate communication skills greatly enhances and contributes to successful relationships. Enormous benefits are derived from communication that is respectful, understandable, instructional, affirmative and, most of all, genuine.

Authentic Communication

With a strong character foundation based on sound principles and values, the opportunity exists for communication that is sincere, intimate, reliable and effective. Authentic communication that's NOT based on manipulation, coercion, or approval.

One can possess tremendous skills and techniques in the art of communication and certainly be somewhat successful. However, without authenticity, the techniques seem shallow. Early in my career, I studied diligently the techniques and skills of persuasive communication and found I was generally able to accomplish what was needed to affect people and get what I wanted. Despite this apparent success, I felt like it was all a hoax, that I was putting something over on those affected. Even my "kindness" was theatrical. Eventually, this false service wore me down and "burn out" settled in.

Only when I established a more substantial character with value oriented principles did I begin to achieve real success from interacting with others. I no longer felt manipulative, but felt a certain calm when receiving the wonderful blessing that comes from sincerely and genuinely assisting others in the accomplishment of their goals. Persuasion techniques, tact and eloquence are most effective when they're used to reinforce the benefits of effective and authentic communication.

Listen Until You See

Successful communicators tell us that listening is the foundation for effective communication. Without listening, one cannot first understand. Without first understanding, one can not likely be understood. In other words, we must first listen with empathy to the other person. LISTEN as if you are unable to respond until you SEE the other person's view. If you are not certain of understanding, restate their position and ask for clarification or confirmation. Therapists call this mirroring. Once you understand, you can then communicate your viewpoint from a perspective that will lead to mutual understanding.

Most of us are so busy trying to "relate" by reading our own biography into someone else's experience or circumstance, or preparing an eloquent response, we never fully understand. Usually without knowing, we either make a judgement, try to analyze their motives, or "fix" them. All from our own perspective and before we have a real understanding of what is being said.

Understanding does not mean we have to agree with someone's position or viewpoint. Maintaining our viewpoint, if it has merit, is critical. Understanding first merely means we see their side and APPRECIATE exactly where they are coming from, how they got there and what triggers their motivation. With that understanding, we can be much more effective in providing an acceptable response or seeking a third alternative.

Effective communication requires an attitude of cooperation, a willingness to find solutions. And, healthy communication requires a respect for boundaries. Deprivation, manipulation, coercion, rage, and avoidance demonstrate a lack of respect for boundaries. These behaviors are usually initiated when reason and understanding are absent.

Yes and No

Many of us have old scripts that keep us from saying Yes when appropriate or No when appropriate. Learn to say Yes. Learn to say No. They're both okay under the right circumstances. When we can't say yes, we often deprive ourselves of good experiences. When we can't say no, we often find ourselves in bad experiences. And, generally, we KNOW when to say No. It simply requires that we be honest with ourselves.

The Great Pause

A large part of our theme for living is centered on the recognition and use of choices. But, because we have choices doesn't mean we will be perfect in our choices. Yet, when choosing a response to a particular circumstance, there is a way to put the odds in our favor.

The benefit of freedom of choice is not just in choosing the action to take, but in choosing the reaction or response to stimulus.

Many renowned communicators have commented on the "opportunity gap" between stimulus and response, and that the key to our success and happiness is how we use that space, or pause. Without doubt, to achieve serenity and put the odds for success in our favor, it is beneficial to contemplate that "great pause" between stimulus and response. Doing so, we discover it's not so much the events in our lives that bring change but the space between events. Except in certain emergency situations, we almost always have the choice to draw on that space between stimulus and our response. It's okay to say things like, "I'll take that into consideration and get back to you tomorrow", or "You've given me something to think about, I'll get back to you", or "That may have some possibilities, I'll think about it and get back to you". All of these responses generate time to "pause" and calculate a response beneficial to the success of the endeavor.

Even when under extreme pressure for a decision, I find it very effective to say "Your position is very strong and persuasive, but I will need just a little time to process my thoughts and consider the consequences. I'll get back to you tomorrow." Once again, we recognize that taking advantage of healthy boundaries and acknowledging our right to choose can lead to higher levels of success and serenity.

Just Ask

To enjoy the process of success and serenity, we can learn to ask for what we need or want. Many of us grew up thinking that "they" should know what we need. When we merely "expect" to get something, and no one else knows we have this expectation, we're surprised or angry when we don't get it. I was like that. Then someone pointed out that I don't read minds well. Neither do most of the people with whom I associate. To my dismay, they can't read my mind even after knowing me for quite some time. Therefore, I must ask for what I need. I must communicate my needs. It doesn't get more difficult than that. If I'm afraid to ask, I may need to examine my fears to see if they are based on old scripts. If so, then I'm expecting old responses. This...is a new day.

Constructive Confrontation

In our effort to communicate effectively, it's beneficial to learn proper participation in conflict or confrontation. We free ourselves to grow when we participate without unmanageable fear, without timidity or unhealthy aggression. Many of us learned that confrontation led to extremes...either rage or complete isolation. Feelings were either expressed inappropriately or just "stuffed" in silence. Conflict does not have to mean abandonment or physical or emotional danger.

One of the best ways to confront someone is to express your feelings using the words, "When you..., I feel.... . For example, "When you don't return my calls, I feel like you don't really care about this project." This concept allows a genuine expression regarding a specific behavior that causes discomfort. This can be communicated without being accusatory or manipulative. Most people find it difficult to "argue" with real feelings. If they do, you can again establish boundaries, "When you don't appreciate my concerns, I feel like I don't count." Usually, you can follow your initial comments with a request that the behavior be stopped. "Please don't ignore my requests for support." This simple technique is incredibly effective in both personal and professional circumstances. When effective communication skills are applied with respect for principles and boundaries, confrontation can lead to resolution, success...and serenity.

Public vs. Personal Success

One of the more significant lessons I've learned (the hard way) is that success in public or professional life is achieved differently than success in personal life. Public relationships require different behaviors than personal relationships. Though this may sound simplistic and easy to understand, it isn't. I, for one, carried most behaviors from one aspect of my life to another. I thought the skills that contributed to my success at work would apply in my personal life. I was not "conscious" about the difference. Here it is:

Public relationships require management; Personal relationships require freedom.

Public or organizational relationships must have management and order to get things done. Many obsessive or "controlling" behaviors are, in fact, effective in the work environment. Many of the really great accomplishments in the world come from obsessive and perfectionistic people. Control of a negotiation or transaction is highly desirable. Management of people, policies, procedures and production is necessary. If management is lackadaisical or without direction, little will get done and the achievement of established goals will be either non-existent or long in coming.

On the other hand, personal relationships deserve and need freedom. The actual control of another person in a personal relationship doesn't work well.

When we attempt to control, we often alienate ourselves from the ones to whom we want to relate. In personal matters, control leads to an effort to manipulate or "fix" another person. The moment we begin to control another in an emotional relationship, we begin to lose them. There is just too much at stake for someone to allow themselves to be controlled at an emotional or personal level. They would give up their treasured self. They would give up their identity to be "like you want" or to take care of your feelings. They give up themselves and become dependent which usually means somebody in the relationship "disappears". The allure, mystery and charm of the relationship disappears. It's a myth that one plus one equals a stronger "one". Though united, it still equals two.

Freedom in a personal relationship does allow us to express our feelings and preferences. And the events and activities involved in daily life may need some direction or order. But, trying to change someone else's behavior is risky business. Just think of the relationships that have been destroyed by trying to fix someone's habits, patterns and behavior. When you feel the need to try to change someone else, try to remember how difficult it is to change your own habits, thinking or behavior. Those kinds of changes must come from within and from a higher Power.

Change is an individual process.
You can't change anyone else.
No one else can change you.
You can explain, demonstrate, ask,
say please, command, demand,
manipulate, abandon, return,
expect, love, hate, cajole,
give and take.
But you can't change someone else.
Oh, but if you let go,
sometimes
someone will change.

We, as part of the whole, must allow others to maintain their own identity, to claim themselves and have the freedom to choose.

Undoubtedly, these concepts of public and personal relationships overlap. But without the awareness that certain relationships require different behaviors, we may tend to treat all relationships or all circumstances the same. We may act out learned behaviors from old scripts regardless of the circumstances and the relationship. This will not only be a roadblock to success, but will deny us our personal peace.

Getting to Know You

Flirting with serenity comes from developing healthy communication with yourself. Developing a personal theme for living includes taking time to get acquainted with yourself. In his book, *Taming Your Gremlin*, Richard Carson talks about "simply noticing" your feelings, your responses and your emotions. As stated previously, many of us did not learn to feel our own feelings, to look within, to acknowledge our worthiness. Now would be a good time to "simply notice" who you are.

Calculated Life Management

This book isn't meant to be an in depth, clinical examination of behavioral guidelines or rules for achievement and spirituality. It's about Calculated Life Management (CLM). The word calculate, is not used in the negative or conniving sense here, but rather as a term for planned, deliberate examination of the choices, alternatives and responses to circumstances.

To achieve success as we understand it requires that we arrange a world in which behavior that is important to us has the best probability to actually occur. By being consciously aware of the conditions or circumstances under which we live best and by making every effort to maintain those conditions, we can maximize the effectiveness and frequency of the behavior that's important to us. It's a matter of putting the odds in our favor by choosing people, places, experiences and behaviors that afford us the best possibility to succeed.

Few people make it out of the ghettos because it takes such a tremendous effort; an effort that requires a real awareness of the choices and does not make an excuse about the "traps" of the surroundings, the people, or the family, but recognizes that the circumstances can be changed. It takes an effort to recognize when the odds for success are less than ideal, and to choose to put the odds for success in our favor. Many of us choose to live in mental or emotional ghettos. We must choose to escape!

Recognize that we have a choice about our personal environment. We can consciously choose to surround ourselves with what we want to be. Cervantes said, "Tell me what company you keep and I'll tell you who you are." Choosing successful people to learn from, model and emulate is productive. Author Napoleon Hill refers to your "Master Mind"; a group comprised of safe, reliable, achievement-oriented people that can support you during your life. Usually, this is a group of five or six, including two or three particularly close relationships that will help you achieve your personal goals. They can be business relationships, friends, advisors and family. You choose them. Of course, it wouldn't be prudent to ignore support or help from outside your Master Mind, but those within will provide most of the reliable support.

When talking of serenity, we keep coming back to the importance of choices. With five billion people on this planet, the circumstances and experiences created by the interaction of these people is infinite, and therefore the choices for each individual are infinite.

By making a choice, we thrust ourselves toward one of many life experiences available to us, or one of many alternate futures. When we choose, we create a new set of changing circumstances involving other people making choices. The possibilities are awesome! However, as a reminder, we need not get too wrapped up in the possibilities, or frozen with fear. Just gather our resources, calculate the best course, given the available information, choose and flow.

Seldom, if ever, does one have to say, "there is nothing I can do." Though sometimes, what we can "do" is trust our choices, let go and let our spirituality take over. Choices are freedom. By limiting our choices, we limit our freedom to choose success and peace of mind. These limitations often hinder us when we are not aware of our behavioral foundation. This requires a spiritual maturity that comes from the practice of the principles and concepts we have examined and an awareness of what author Stephen Covey calls "the Maturity Continuum".

When first born, we are dependent. This means that I look to *you* for responsibility. I look to you to take care of me, support me, make me feel good, be responsible for everything that happens to me. Many people that don't mature past this state often feel like victims. If *you* don't come through for me, I blame *you*.

Some of us achieve a little more maturity and discover that we can be independent. This means I look to *me* for the responsibility. I can do it. I only rely on *me*. If it goes wrong, it's all about me. Sometimes these people find themselves overwhelmed with being a martyr and have difficulty delegating and exercising prudent management practices that permit growth in both their business and personal life. After all, it's quite a god-like place to put yourself in to be responsible for "everything". The unhealthy part of the dependent and independent system is that, without healthy self-esteem, proper boundaries and balance, we find ourselves with self-generated anxiety and feeling very distanced from others. It's not a place of serenity.

Though there are appropriate times for both dependence and independence, the most mature position is one that says *we* can do it ... a state of maximum effectiveness called interdependence. If we cooperate, communicate, combine our strengths, gifts, skills and experience, we can accomplish our goals. We can freely seek the third alternative without risk to our psyche and discover something closer to optimum excellence.

Declaration of Interdependence

To wink at success and flirt with serenity, we embrace a Declaration of Interdependence that says though I am self-reliant, competent and responsible, so are you and that *together*, we can accomplish things that neither of us might accomplish without the other. If I'm emotionally involved, I can choose to find a great sense of worth within myself, but recognize that true interdependence requires loving and giving to others and receiving love from others. This concept accepts that both *you and I* have resources that can be meaningful to both of us and those resources properly activated can take us to greater moments.

Energy

The intent of this book is to discover a gentle way to examine the path to success and serenity. Our efforts to succeed are enclosed in an envelope of ambition sealed with a soft kiss of self-acceptance. With the many tools discussed here, we can perhaps live a more balanced life that will allow the things we want to come.

However, little can be accomplished without initiative. Whether our actions are of a "doing" or "spiritual" nature, we must act. We may have more knowledge and we may be more aware, but without application, knowledge and awareness do not equal power. True power is applied knowledge. This can only come from an energy we find within that empowers us physically, mentally, emotionally and spiritually. While we may not have all the energy we need all the time,

*Personal success
is dependent on our willingness
to energize a particular
circumstance or experience
with appropriate actions and
responses that will put the odds
in our favor
for getting the result
we desire.*

It takes personal energy to achieve personal peace. When we generate the energy to be willing, we have indeed, succeeded. Serenity will arrive on time.

And So

Wink at Success, Flirt with Serenity is a comfortable concept for those seeking a way to live that harmonizes with both their own desire for achievement and the natural way of the universe. We move with the winds of change while growing toward a balanced state of success that exudes personal peace. The concepts and guidelines contained in this book are not absolute and represent only doorways to your personal opportunity for success and serenity. In some cases, the doors are left open for your interpretation and experimentation. Remember choice....

The Final Notion

There is one more notion that I would like to share that I sincerely hope will occasionally invade your quest for personal success and peace. This simple notion is to *"lighten up!" Don't be so together you fall apart.* Listen to the music and dance to the song of life!

There are golden moments!
They are going on
now!

Wink At Success, Flirt With Serenity

Affirmation

Today, I give myself permission
to claim success.
I choose success,
regardless of my past.
I believe in myself.
I embrace serenity as I flow
with the everchanging circumstances
that define Life and trust that a greater
Power will safely guide my journey.
I am willing to make choices
that create a future of health,
prosperity, love and peace.
I am worth it.

Thank You

I'm glad and grateful you chose to explore the concepts of success and serenity with me. For me, this exploration continues because what I have shared with you, I am still learning...

My wish for you is that your life's journey will lead to discoveries providing extraordinary awareness and profound personal success, spirituality and peace. As you make these discoveries, I encourage you to share them with the rest of us. We need your contribution and your sharing will enhance our journey, ultimately bringing us all closer to each other.

Suggested Reading

Illusions, Richard Bach

One, Richard Bach

Awakening the Giant Within, Anthony Robbins

The 7 Habits of Highly Effective People, Stephen Covey

Oh, the Places You'll Go, Dr. Suess

Taming Your Gremlin, Richard Carson

The Richest Man in Babylon, George S. Clason

Healing the Shame That Binds You, John Bradshaw

Passages, Gail Sheehan

The Road Less Traveled, M. Scott Peck

Handbook to Higher Consciousness, Ken Keyes, Jr.

Necessary Losses, Judith Viorst

From Love That Hurts to Love That's Real, Sylvia Peterson

Getting the Love You Want, Harville Hendrix

Co-dependent No More, Melody Beattie

Boundaries, Anne Katherine